Be Silent or Be Killed

A Scottish banker under siege in Mumbai's terrorist attacks

ROGER HUNT

Luath Press Limited

EDINBURGH

www.luath.co.uk

First published 2010 by Corskie Press
This edition 2011

ISBN: 978-1906817-76-3

The paper used in this book is recyclable. It is made from
low-chlorine pulps produced in a low-energy, low-emissions
manner from renewable forests.

Printed and bound by CPI Antony Rowe, Chippenham

Typeset in 11 point Sabon

To Irene, Lisa, Christopher and Stephanie

And in memory of all those who lost their lives
in the 26 November 2008 terrorist attacks in Mumbai

Contents

ACKNOWLEDGEMENTS

I'VE WRITTEN THIS BOOK for a reason. It's part of my own process of coming to terms with being caught in what was known as India's 9/11. Why did I live when so many other people died? I'm sure it's a question that runs through the mind of all survivors of a major catastrophe.

I wanted my family, friends and colleagues to understand a bit more about my perilous position in Mumbai between late on Wednesday 26 November 2008 until the afternoon of Friday 28 November. I've been asked so often about the situation, I thought it best to simply tell the tale, as it happened, without frills or embellishment. In particular, I knew that my children were keen to know what happened to me. Yet, it never felt that there was a right time – or indeed way – of sharing the details. Writing a book would give them the chance to know and understand every detail at a time that suited them individually.

Above all, I also wanted people to know that they played a significant role too. There were many friends and colleagues who worked hard to keep me alive, raise my spirits and get me back home safely. So I would like to thank them for making this true story possible and for the part that each and every one of them played in ensuring that I returned home safe to my family, my second chance at life.

I'd liked to thank MI5, Hostage and Crisis Negotiation Unit, and the Black Cats – to whom I owe my life.

At RBS Gogarburn in Edinburgh, Lynne Highway, Acting HR Director, Andrew Sharman, Pete Philp, Lesley Laird, Karlynn Sokoluk, Lorraine Kneebone, Stan Hosie, Incident Management, my other senior colleagues in Policy & Advice Services and the many colleagues who supported me upon my return to work. A huge thank you also goes to Gavin Reid, the RBS man in Mumbai, for providing me with a safe haven upon my release and escorting me every inch of the way back from India to Scotland.

In Macduff, I would like to thank our family and friends for their vital support both during and after the terror attacks. They have been a great source of support and comfort and a major part of the healing process for myself, Irene and our children. In particular Abby, Irene's dad, and her sisters Karine and Carole. A great deal of thanks is also due to the staff at Macduff Primary School for all of their support both during Irene's absence and return to work.

I'd also like to thank Frank Docherty, of Career Associates in Edinburgh, who introduced me to the writer and journalist Kenny Kemp. Kenny has spent time with me and Irene turning my taped thoughts into a proper and compelling narrative. In addition to benefiting from his professional writing skills we have also acquired a great friend. I am also grateful for support from Jennie Renton and Dave Gilchrist in the completion of my book.

Finally, a message to any unfortunate person who finds themselves in a situation similar to mine: *No matter how difficult the circumstances you find yourself in, when all may seem lost, never ever give up.*

Roger Hunt
June 2010

FOREWORD

HARDLY A DAY goes by without some terrorist atrocity hitting the headlines around the world. The death tolls vary, but these barbaric acts always involve the slaughter and maiming of innocent human beings. London. Moscow. Madrid. Kabul. Karachi. New York. And then there was Mumbai. For a few days towards the end of 2008, India's financial and commercial centre was in the full glare of the world's media spotlight as a brutal life and death struggle unfolded on our television screens.

Roger Hunt was caught up in the killing. And he survived. Just. Roger is a regular guy from the North East of Scotland. He and his wife, Irene, and family are hard-working Scots who want to enjoy their lives. They have never gone looking for fame or the limelight. But life throws up so many different paths.

When Roger became involved in the Mumbai terrorist attacks in November 2008, he was put to the ultimate test. For two days, his life hung on a thin piece of thread – and he was forced to make calculated decisions that would ultimately save his skin.

Roger Hunt's story is a tale of our modern 21st century times. It is about how individuals become wrapped up in our increasing global world. It is about raw fear and dangerous uncertainty; about resilience, common sense and calmness; and, ultimately, about the sustaining power of love.

For those who say Roger should never have been in India in the first place there is one important point to be made. For generations, Scots have gone around the world on business and for commercial reasons. As a small nation, it's an ingrained part of our intrepid character. Roger Hunt was simply doing his job with the Royal Bank of Scotland.

And here there is another central aspect to this story. Roger's developing career came about because RBS was growing into one of the world's leading banks. This created opportunities and challenges, and Roger's story is played out against this and the wider backdrop of the international banking crisis of October 2008, which led to the collapse of RBS and its bail-out by the British taxpayer to the tune of 45.5 billion pounds.

If there is a message, it is that those who seek to kill and maim innocent people with machine guns and bombs must not be allowed to prevail.

Roger Hunt came out of this with a great admiration for the people of India and how they coped with the tragedy: he salutes their spirit and resolve. He knows how lucky he is to have survived to tell his remarkable tale. He tells it as it happened with no frills and no exaggeration: simply, the honest truth.

Kenny Kemp
June 2010

CHAPTER ONE

My Own Mumbai Horror

MY HEART WAS POUNDING through my ribcage. After hour upon hour of silence, broken only by intermittent machine gun fire and exploding grenades, there was a violent crash in the hotel room next door.

For 60 hours without sleep, as tiredness crept in, my senses had been in an acute state of crisis – especially my hearing. Now my pulse quickened. I sat up and strained my ears as the noise next door increased and I heard muffled shouts. Then silence. I was listening for even the faintest creak on the floor. Outside the window, the crows croaked and cackled as they circled in the air.

An instruction was barked out and then another voice called out in fear. This must be the attackers systematically 'clearing' each room, I thought, and imagined them murdering the defenceless occupants.

For 15 long minutes I strained to listen. Petrified as never before, I made not a sound. Then I heard scuffling right outside my door. This was it. It was all over for me. I took a deep breath of air gritty with smoke. Was I about to be blasted to kingdom come, was there any chance my ordeal would end in release and a return to freedom?

Earlier I had dragged the brown leather couch into a corner, then I had climbed in behind it and crouched down out of sight. I had been in this position for nearly two days, without eating, drinking or visiting the toilet. I had been lying so long on my side that my right arm was completely numb and I couldn't move it. The cramped position was also very painful... but adrenalin overcame any injury when I heard a voice shout:

'Open the door! Open the door!'

As a band of terrorists swept across Mumbai, I had been pinned down in this room on the 14th floor of the Oberoi Hotel for two days. My tactics had been to lie low – literally – and if it came to it, conceal my identity. I had witnessed the killers slaughtering my fellow guests in the foyer. I had listened as these murderers moved from room to room, shooting any Western visitors they discovered. I stuck to my plan to stay in hiding and not attract any attention, even as a fire gripped the hotel and smoke made it difficult to breathe.

But now surely it was my turn. Even if the men in the corridor were friendly forces here to rescue me I didn't want to take a chance. I had been using my Blackberry to communicate with the outside world and I'd been advised that if this happened, I should stand up with my arms raised. But my sense of survival overruled this.

My mind was racing: what if this was the terrorists and not a rescue party? If I followed this instruction, I was going to give them an easy target. There was no doubt these ruthless gunmen would kill me.

There was a terrific crash and the heavy wooden door burst open. Still cowering behind the large settee, which acted as a sort of barricade, I could hear quick and heavy footsteps sweeping into the room, and then the click, clack of metallic weapons. I heard the safety catches of automatic weapons clicked off. And then the curtains were pulled back and brightness invaded the fetid darkness.

If this was the killers, my time was up – and equally, if this was the Indian Black Cat commandos, any sudden movement from me now might cause them to open fire in panic.

I was caught between life and death and the problem of how to reveal myself to the strangers in my room. I'd kept a small knife beside me. But it would be useless against a machine gun, so I slid it under the couch and yelled, 'Please don't shoot!'

The barrel of a sub-machine gun came prodding over the top of the couch. I tried to pull myself up – but my right arm was so numb I couldn't get it into the air. The three armed men wore dark clothing, without markings – as had the death squad I had seen two days earlier blasting away the diners in the Tiffin and Kandahar restaurants downstairs.

Very shakily, I just about managed to stand, when a hand gripped me and pushed me back against the wall. I was almost too exhausted to care, but panic surged through my body. I believed this was my final moment on earth.

They say your life passes through your mind when you are about to die, and I suppose it's true – all I thought about was my wife and children, and how they are my life. Here I was, thousands of miles away from home in Macduff in the North East of Scotland, caught up in a major terrorist event in Mumbai. This Indian hotel was not the place I wanted to die.

This experience has given me a different perspective. I will never again take comfort and an easy existence for granted; I now fully appreciate the importance of family, friends and loyal work colleagues. In the West, it's all too easy to put out of our minds the vast gulf between rich and poor, how the world of the 'haves' is so starkly paralleled by that of the 'have-nots'.

Most of my working life I was oblivious to this parallel

world. I had my wake-up call in November 2008. Working for the Royal Bank of Scotland, I was on a second business trip to India where I was helping to set up a new operation. I was fortunate to survive one of the most audacious terrorist attacks in recent times.

My story is a personal one. I'm not a politician, a media celebrity or even a senior bank director, but I have been encouraged to tell my true story. It is how I became caught up in the Mumbai massacres, and witnessed the slaughter of innocent people who happened to be in the wrong place at the wrong time.

For over 40 hours, I was a hostage in a burning hotel while a group of suicidal terrorists – who had already murdered hotel workers and guests in cold blood – remained barricaded in with hostages on the floor directly above me.

As the machine gun fire, rifle bullets, grenades and a bomb crumped into the building, I was kept alive by my Blackberry contact with the outside world, especially my amazing Royal Bank colleagues back in the Edinburgh headquarters. As the intensity of the gunfire and grenade attacks increased, I concluded that it was unlikely that I would survive. I thought of Irene, my wife, and my children, Lisa, Christopher and Stephanie, and all the things I'd never said to them. I also thought of my poor parents, who would hear of my violent death – and how this would rekindle the pain of the loss of my brother, Christopher, who died, a 16-year-old deck hand, in a Highland fishing boat disaster in December 1985.

Many people will recall the horror of the picture of the 'Man Who Jumped' after the September 11 atrocities in the United States in 2001. The man falling from the north tower of the burning World Trade Centre in New York was an image I could not erase from my brain as I trembled in that blackened hotel room. It was this horrific image that prevented me from jumping. As I contemplated my own fate, a powerful, almost primal, instinct to survive kicked in. Somehow I discovered a clarity and calmness of thinking which helped me make the right decisions under extreme pressure. This, coupled with luck – or perhaps fate – meant I survived to tell the tale, where so many others perished.

CHAPTER TWO

Finding My Anchor

TO UNDERSTAND WHAT I mean about parallel lives, I think it's important to know about my own upbringing and what has moulded and shaped me. My early years were pretty normal, although, as I will explain later, there was some terrible family grief that we had to come to terms with. I was born in Banff, on the North East coast of Scotland, on 10 March 1966. The rugged Moray Firth coastline weaves west to east along from Buckie to Fraserburgh and then turns down south to Peterhead. Along this North Sea coast are a string of fishing communities, including Whitehills, where I lived as a youngster, and my own home town of Macduff. To this day, it's an area that places a great deal of store in the value of ordinary people and community, and the hard work of honest folk.

My dad, also called Roger, worked in the building trade, and when I was about three we moved to Glenrothes. It was a new town in Fife and there was the promise of more work and opportunity. But the pull of the North East of Scotland was always too much for the family. One night, when I was ten, we packed all our belongings in a car and moved back to Whitehills.

I left behind some Fife chums without saying goodbye that I never saw again, although years later I looked up some of them.

I went to Fordyce Primary School until I was 12 and worked hard as a student, as I was ambitious from a young age.

At school we were all fanatical about football. I played almost every day and was fairly good but never had the build to be a strong player. But my brothers and I loved going to the big games and especially to Aberdeen FC – the Dons – who played at Pittodrie Stadium 45 miles away. I was the eldest of four children and from 12 years of age onwards, when I went to secondary school, Raymond, Christopher and myself would go on the bus to the home games at Pittodrie to watch one of the greatest teams that has emerged from Scottish football. My sister, Lynne, wasn't so fanatical on football.

For a few seasons we never missed a home match: it was an amazing team. With my dad struggling to find good employment our family wasn't well off, so I had to find a job. I started as a delivery boy on a milk round with Robertson's dairy in Macduff.

Winter mornings in the North East are often icy and dark. My work began at 5am, so I pulled on my warmest clothes, scarf, jacket and boots. Fred, the regular milk van driver, would pick me up. He was always right on time and I came to admire his cheery disposition and his ability to get up on the darkest and coldest mornings – even when the milk bottles were frozen – and do the job. It all seemed so much safer and more trustworthy then. At many of the houses where we delivered the milk, the residents were still asleep. They would leave the weekly money on a table or in a kitchen drawer. I used to tip-toe in, take the cash, and leave the milk with the household still slumbering.

Most of the major events in my teenage life revolved around Saturday nights out with my mates in Macduff, Banff and Whitehills and travelling to watch 'The Fabulous Dons'. In 1982, Aberdeen were playing in the preliminary rounds of the

European Cup Winners' Cup. It was an amazing evening and the Dons ran out winners 7–0 against FC Sion of Switzerland. Little did any of us know about what was to come.

Under manager Alex Ferguson, 'Fergie', the Dons were the best Scottish football team of that era, better even than the 'Old Firm' of Glasgow Celtic and Rangers. Aberdeen won the Scottish League championship twice and the Scottish Cup three times, in 1982, 1983 and 1984. The whole team was packed with legends: Jim Leighton, Doug Rougvie, Alex McLeish, Peter Weir, John McMaster, Willie Miller, Gordon Strachan, Ian Scanlon, Steve Archibald, Mark McGhee, Neil Simpson, John Hewitt, Eric Black and Neale Cooper: every one was a hero to me.

They were a brilliant team with an amazing attitude. This was infectious and we loved being part of the Red Army of supporters who shouted, cheered and sang for our team. The bus from the Banff branch of the Aberdeen FC Supporters' Club would leave the town at 11am and drop us off at the Bobbin Mill pub in King Street. The older guys would go for a lager or two while we'd walk to the ground. Such was the clamour to see this great side, if you didn't have a season ticket, you simply didn't get in.

Fergie was the boss and he was still learning his trade as a football coach. Over the years in my professional life I have come to admire Sir Alex, the Manchester United boss since 1986, as a supreme coach. He knows how to mould and motivate a group of thoroughbred and often wayward young people and allow them to perform at their optimum level. His motto of: *Never Say Die, Never Give Up* has been inspirational to me.

Working alongside Fred the milkman instilled in me a work ethic, and watching the Dons in the 1980s taught me about the value of team-work – and since then I've often thought sporting achievement and success remains a powerful metaphor for life as well as business. I still think business can learn a lot from examining the very best sporting coaches.

I worked hard at school, although I wasn't a swot. I was dux (top of the academic class) at Fordyce Primary and was made a prefect at Banff Academy. I had an idea that I wanted to be a lawyer. I took six Highers in fifth year and gained the qualifications to get into Aberdeen, Edinburgh or Glasgow universities. But the reality of coming from a working-class background struck home. I knew it wasn't financially viable for me to go to university, and it was better to go and find a job.

When I was 15 I started seeing a local girl called Irene, who was attractive and rather shy, but very neat and well organised. Her dad was a hugely charismatic fishing skipper who had two boats that went out to fish from Macduff. The fishing is embedded into the life of the North East coast. It's an extremely harsh and dangerous way to eke out a living. For Radio Four listeners tucked up in the bedrooms of our big cities the names listed on the Met Office shipping forecast – Viking, North Utsire, South Utsire, Forties, Cromarty, etc – might seem an irrelevance; but these forecasts were of vital practical use for our fishermen, whose voyages took them to Bailey, Hebrides, Fair Isle, south Iceland and far out into the storm-lashed Atlantic. Between 1961 and 1980 there were 909 recorded deaths at sea involving fishermen. The weather and the conditions at sea are a daily topic of conversation in fishing communities and every time the boats go to sea, there are fears in the back of the mind of all left on shore.

While I wanted to start working, I didn't really want to go to sea. So I sent my CV and a covering letter to a number of banks who were looking for school leavers and I was accepted by the Trustee Savings Bank group, later Lloyds TSB, and also by the Royal Bank of Scotland. I took the Royal Bank job because it offered better prospects. It was a decision which gave me nearly 26 good years as a banker.

On Wednesday 11 May 1983, Aberdeen won the European Cup Winners' Cup, beating Real Madrid 2–1 in Gothenburg. Eric Black opened the scoring while the Spaniards equalised with a penalty. The game went to extra time and John Hewitt scored the winner. The whole of the North East of Scotland went wild. The returning heroes celebrated in an open-top bus along Aberdeen's Union Street. It was an epic summer in the North East.

What a good year that was for me. On 18 July 1983, aged 17, I began my career in banking. I was told to report to the training centre in Kilgraston Road, the Grange, in the leafy south side of Edinburgh. It was the first time I'd been away from home on my own. The bank seemed very formal, partly because of its awesome tradition. The Royal Bank of Scotland was founded in 1727, some years after the Bank of Scotland was set up in 1695. Scottish bankers were admired internationally for the acumen and prudence with which they looked after people's money.

I was sent back to work in the Banff branch of the Royal Bank of Scotland. It was all rather repetitive. We counted cheques and cash every night, to ensure that not a penny was missing, and often we'd be there long after closing time to ensure that the books were balanced. Banking hours were 9.30am until 3.30pm, but if there was a mistake we might not get out until nearer 6pm. I wasn't really sure that this was what I wanted to do, so I applied to the police force. I went to Elgin and sat the entrance exam, which I passed, and then I went for a medical at Bucksburn regional headquarters in Aberdeen. During the sight test the doctor asked me to read the letters on the top line of the eye-chart. It was like one of those classic comedy moments. I couldn't even see the chart, never mind the actual letters.

'I'm sorry, I can't read anything,' I said.

'Well, thank you, that will be all,' the doctor replied.

The 30 seconds it took to do that test put paid to any idea I had of joining the police and made me reconsider what I had to do to further my career in the bank.

Most of my pals had gone straight into the fishing when they left school. My salary in the bank was about £50 a week. A 16-year-old returning from a week at sea could end up with £350 in his hand. I began to wonder who the daft one was. So when Irene's dad offered to take me out to sea, I went out on his boat, the *Crystal Waters*, a pair trawler with his son John's boat, the *Crystal Sea*: they would fish with nets slung between the two vessels. The weather wasn't too bad but it was rough enough to make me sick for most of the time. It was a miserable existence standing below deck, gutting cod, haddock, lemon sole and plaice, pouring ice over them and piling up the crates. My fingers were cracked and sore with the bitter cold. The stench of diesel fumes and the constant rocking of the trawler made it very uncomfortable. I'm proud of the North East's trawling heritage and how it binds the communities, but I finished up after this first trip, and, despite the lure of the ready cash, decided that the fishing wasn't for me.

By now, Irene was becoming a major part of my life – and to this day she has remained my single biggest inspiration. She encouraged me to progress with banking, accelerate my training and sit my banking exams. Her dad and mum were also supportive of my decision to pursue banking more seriously as a career. When we were 18 we got engaged and started to save up for our future. She has been the anchor in my life – an appropriate description coming from a seafaring family. Over the years we have done everything together and have been proud of raising our three children: Lisa, Christopher and Stephanie.

In 1984 I was moved to the Fraserburgh branch of the Royal Bank of Scotland. Fraserburgh, known as 'the Broch', was still one of the UK's biggest fishing ports. When the fleet returned with its haul of cod and haddock there was plenty of cash to throw around, and this bank branch was a great place to learn a bit more about real business. From boat financing to asset management, the branch was always busy with customers. There were bills to pay for oil and provisions at sea, new nets or radar kit. The fishing rebates all came in around Christmas with hundreds of thousands of pounds changing hands in the North East.

I had passed my driving test when I was 17 but I still couldn't afford a car. That would have to wait. And because there was no regular bus service from Whitehills to the Broch, I moved into a room rented from a wonderful woman in her 60s called Jean Webster, who worked in Webster's Bakery, on North Street. She lived with her sister, Anne Harrison, and her husband. They were all deeply religious people, closely connected with the Fishermen's Mission, the Christian society which looks after those fisherfolk who have fallen on hard times, or simply need a warm place to stay after a trip to sea. I was expected to observe the house rules, but I think Jean and Annie enjoyed having a young banker living with them. It gave them some kudos to talk about the young 'loon' from the Royal Bank.

My rent was £12 a week, and this was extremely good value because I had about half of Jean's house. And there was another bonus: Webster's Bakery made the best cakes, baps (morning rolls) and butteries (known as rowies) in the Broch. Every Monday night when I'd returned for the week, Jean would knock on the door and give me several bags of baked goodies, which lasted me the week. It was a wonderful place to stay for a while; but I was young and full of ambition.

Three months before I married Irene, I was transferred to Peterhead, then still one the UK's busiest fishing harbours and also a port used by the developing offshore oil and gas industries. My mentor was the senior branch manager, a great guy called Bill Nicol. Bill had a heart of gold. He was an unorthodox fellow, always immaculately turned out in pinstripe suit, tie and braces. A real grafter who instilled in me the importance of doing things properly, he was a stickler for getting it absolutely right – first time. He inculcated an ethic of hard work, trust and honesty in all of us.

Bill, a keen golfer, lived in Aberdeen and travelled up during the week to the branch. I remember him hobbling out of the office with a bad leg one Saturday afternoon before going back home; over that weekend, he had a heart attack and died on the golf course. It was huge loss to the bank.

I've worked with hundreds of talented people but Bill remained my litmus test for what was right. Throughout my career I often asked myself: *How would Bill have done this? What would Bill say about that?*

CHAPTER THREE

Losing a Brother at Sea

TRAGEDY VISITED MY FAMILY on 20 December 1985. My 16-year-old brother Christopher was working as a deck hand on the MFV *Bon Ami* (BF 323) the night it foundered on rocks known as Minister's Point, just a few hundred metres short of the entrance to Kinlochbervie harbour.

That evening had been particularly stormy with the wind bitter and heavy snow falling well into the evening. On such nights I often thought about my brother being out at sea. With Irene's side of the family so heavily involved in the fishing industry and most of my school friends now at the fishing, I was so familiar with that way of life that I never had any real fears for his safety. Perhaps it's superstitious – many people who make their living by fishing are that way. And after all, Christopher was berthed with a skipper who had years of experience and was very well respected in the community. If anything, it seemed as if Christopher had pretty much landed on his feet in securing a position on the *Bon Ami*. I had visions of him making lots of money, driving a sporty car and buying expensive gifts at birthdays, Christmas and anniversaries.

Christopher had initially been given his chance in the summer of 1985 on the sister boat, the *Bon Accord*, owned by the same skipper, and had enjoyed his early months at the fishing. Although on an apprentice's wage, the money he was making was reasonable given that he was still at home with my mum and dad. When I returned home from Fraserburgh at weekends, you could often find him in the Cutty Sark, one of two pubs in Whitehills, where he loved to play pool, and on many occasions picked up a trophy or prize money for his efforts. Strictly speaking he shouldn't have been allowed in because he was only 16 at the time.

It was commonplace for fishing boats to have a number of relatives aboard the same vessel, which was ideal for many families when the fishing was going well. But the other side of the coin was the loss of several members of a single family when a tragedy occurred. Christopher had worked really well on the *Bon Accord* and was good friends with the skipper's son, who was berthed on the *Bon Ami*. Then before Christmas, the skipper made the decision to swap the lads and put Christopher onto his boat.

On the *Bon Accord* he had built up a strong bond with the crew, but things were different on the *Bon Ami*. He didn't seem settled. On one occasion, after a long hard trip out into the Atlantic, Chris had just walked in the door when he was advised by another crew member that he was required to be on board for 5am to clean the boat's quarters. He was very diligent and turned up on the dot and waited for some time, only to find out it was all a big leg-pull. This was one of a string of so-called practical jokes which started to annoy Chris and he began to question whether fishing was the life that he wanted to pursue. On the last trip of the year before the boats tied up for the festive period, I arrived at my mum and dad's house on the Sunday afternoon to find them in mid-conversation. Chris was fed-up and contemplating phoning up his skipper to say that he had decided not to go to back to sea on the *Bon Ami*. Irene and I listened to the discussions. It just seemed wrong, as Christopher was such a happy-go-lucky individual with a ready smile. Normally, he was exceptionally positive and cheery. I have always lived life with the viewpoint that you cannot change the past, only shape the future, and that there is nothing to be gained in life by having regrets.

As I lay in the silence and deathly darkness of Room 1478 in the Oberoi Hotel in Mumbai, I wondered if I would take to my grave what I had never shared with anyone: that I did have one major regret in life. I know in my heart that Christopher had already made up his mind that he was not going to sail that Sunday and the relaxed tone of the conversation in the house suggested that my parents were not keen to persuade him otherwise. If only I had known the consequences of stepping in and convincing him that with it so close to Christmas this would be the last trip of the year; he would then have a couple of weeks off to think things through before making such a big decision.

He obviously respected my point of view: I was his big brother, after all. I convinced him to go back to the sea once more. He picked up his bag and I drove him down to the harbour and dropped him off. As he headed off, little did I know that this was the last time that I would see him and that within a couple of weeks our lives would be absolutely shattered. I have learned to live with the fact that he is gone, and even the fact that he was taken, along with his fellow crew-mates and skipper, in such cruel circumstances and at such a young age. Technically he was little more than a boy, but in our eyes, every ounce a man. I have however also carried the hurt within for almost 24 years that it could all have been so different had I not reasoned with him to make the final trip. This is, and remains, my only regret in life.

On 20 December I was awoken by my radio alarm clock, which had been set on the local Northsound station. As I rose from my bed, the newsreader's urgent voice blurbed out: '*The North East is waking today to the news of another fishing tragedy. It is reported that the Banff registered* Bon Ami *has been lost…*' The signal wasn't great. I tried frantically to turn the radio dial to pick up better reception, hoping with all of my heart that I had somehow misheard the newsreader and that this news was not accurate. I even clung onto the fact that working in the bank I knew that many fishing vessels had the same name and it may have been the port of registry that they had got wrong; in a really selfish way it almost felt acceptable to understand that a boat had been lost as long as it was not the one that my brother was on.

There were no mobile phones in these days and my landlady's house did not have a phone. I turned on the small portable television in my room to see if I could get any more news. It was absolutely freezing that morning but I felt nothing. In a state of shocked disbelief, I started to get dressed when I heard a knock at the front door. It was my uncle Benny, who had made the short trip by car down to my Fraserburgh lodgings to collect me.

A giant of a man, Benny filled the small door frame. When I asked him if what I had heard on the radio was true, there was no mistaking the look in his eyes.

'Chris is gone, Rog,' he said with a peculiar softness in his voice that I had never heard before.

I felt the tightest of knots in my stomach and I went exceptionally quiet. I never uttered another word, simply taking a few minutes to gather together a few belongings from North Street before heading back to Whitehills.

It must have been an impossibly difficult journey for my uncle. We travelled almost half of the 20 miles before I spoke with him again.

'Do you think it's possible Chris might have managed to scramble to shore and he's just not been picked up yet?' I murmured.

Benny's expression as he wrestled with how to put it spoke volumes. He slowed the car and looked over at me.

'There was no hope for him, and there were no survivors,' he said.

His tone was caring and gentle but the message was definitive.

My grandfather had passed away when I was 17. Other than that, I had never experienced the death of someone I loved. As we headed to Whitehills, the memory of grandad's coffin being carried from the house intensified my sense of loss.

My brother was gone and I was never going to see him again.

This was impossible to comprehend. I couldn't cry. I just stared ahead at the road wondering what had happened and if he had suffered. The more I thought about the cruel sea, the more the knot in my stomach tightened.

Soon we drew into the street where my parents lived. There were already a number of cars outside their house and I braced myself for meeting everyone.

Still unable to shed a tear, I hugged my mum, then my dad. Dad's style was pretty undemonstrative and this was the first time, as far as I can recall, that we ever embraced, though our childhood had been happy and we four children had always felt secure in the love of both parents who had always cared for us very well, despite having very little materially.

Now dad squeezed me tight and sobbed into my ear, 'Chris is gone, Rog. What are we going to do without him?'

I had never seen him in tears and it was this that finally

brought a stream to my own cheeks. My only sister, Lynne, was upstairs in her bedroom, devastated by what had happened. But my other brother wasn't there and no one seemed to know where to locate him at this critical moment.

As a family unit we had experienced knock-backs and hardships, but the loss of Christopher was something that all of us struggled to cope with. A Scottish fishing community is something very deep and special. During the day many more family members arrived. The details of the tragedy were starting to unfold. On the evening of 19 December a number of boats from the fleet were making their way back to the port of Kinlochbervie through stormy conditions. One after another they made their way into the safety of the harbour, much to the delight of the crews, who were not only finished their fishing trips, but were now also tied up for the festive season, home for a few weeks. The *Bon Ami* was making her way to port and there were fishing vessels immediately in front, one being the *Bon Accord*, where my brother was once a crew member. As the *Bon Accord* negotiated its way through the waves it realised that there was no sign of the *Bon Ami* behind. The skipper of the *Bon Accord* then received a radio call from the skipper on Christopher's boat to say that he had run aground at Minister's Point and could they come back out and tow them off.

It soon transpired that the situation was far graver than first thought, and a Mayday signal was sent out. That evening everything conspired against the lads on the *Bon Ami*. The weather conditions were so atrocious that every effort to throw a tow rope failed. The risk to the rescue crews was severe. With the *Bon Ami* stuck fast on the rocks and the crew clinging to the deck-rails, some wearing life jackets, others not, the situation was dire.

I still wonder to this day if things would have turned out

differently had Christopher been wearing a life jacket. I also wonder about why there was no rescue helicopter based at Stornoway, on the Isle of Lewis, which potentially could have arrived in time to winch the men to safety. A helicopter had to be scrambled from Lossiemouth, the RAF rescue base on the opposite coast of Scotland. It had to be refuelled before take off, and then had to fly around the Cairngorm Mountains, rather than over them, so it was never destined to reach the lads in time. With the boat now listing badly, and being pounded by the strong seas, the crew, including my brother, grew increasingly desperate. A close friend, later the best man at my wedding, described the minute that everything seemed to stop in silence momentarily, as one huge wave smashed the boat and crew members into the mountainous seas. All six on board perished.

In my grief and anger I later wrote to Margaret Thatcher, the Prime Minister, to raise questions over the provision of search-and-rescue helicopters in the Highlands. She wrote a letter of sympathy on 10 Downing Street notepaper saying that she was investigating locating a service in the North West of Scotland in consultation with the Transport Secretary, HM Coastguard and the UK Search and Rescue Committee. She ended her letter with the words: 'I'm glad you wrote to me personally, though I know how little words can do to help. My thoughts and prayers are with you, your parents and your brother and sister at this sad time.' It was greatly appreciated.

As the day went on and the cruel reality started to crystalise in my mind, I still had no answer as to the whereabouts of my brother Raymond. I needed to get out of the house to clear my head for a short while. I met up with several of my mates in the Cutty Sark. They had all heard about the tragedy and everyone knew some, if not all, of the *Bon Ami* crew. We stood at the bar drinking pints of lager and they did their best to console me. But where was Raymond? It turned out that that very day he had gone off with a young woman he'd fallen in love with. I didn't know how to contact him – and while he was blithely unaware of the crisis, I was left to deal with our grieving parents. This would all return to my mind in the darkest hours of the Mumbai siege.

CHAPTER FOUR

Upwardly Mobile

FOR GENERATIONS, SCOTS had gone to the Indian subcontinent seeking fame, fortune and adventure. My reason for heading to Mumbai was more mundane – progressing my banking career. I wasn't seeking death-defying adventure!

While the British Empire is long gone and India has been an independent democratic nation within the British Commonwealth since 1947 – 20 years before I was born – the cultural and economic bonds between Britain and India remain incredibly powerful.

From 2000 onwards, RBS evolved into one of the world's largest banking forces. I was fortunate in that my own career was on the way up with the meteoric rise of the bank and I was extremely proud of the professionalism of my banking colleagues. So when I heard I had been chosen to work on a project in Mumbai I was elated, although I have to admit my general knowledge of modern India at that time was limited.

Of course, I had the usual Indian stereotypes of a Scot living in a small town in the North East of Scotland. Some might say prejudices, but I've never been that way inclined and I've always extended the hand of friendship to anyone who takes me as they find me. I would say that education and taking the time to understand someone's point of view are the keys to universal harmony. My images of India were carved out from an array of books, television programmes and films: Rudyard Kipling's *Kim*, about the young boy spy who lived in an intrepid time of espionage and intrigue on the north-west frontier; EM Forster's *A Passage to India*, which I studied when I was doing English; the 1980s television series *The Jewel in the Crown*; and Sir Richard Attenborough's film portrayal of Mahatma Gandhi, the iconic Indian figure who challenged the British with his campaign for independence based on non-violence.

More recently, we've seen the confidence and humour of India, through the hilarious exploits of Sanjeev Bhaskar in the *Kumars at No 42* and *Goodness Gracious Me*. I remember the brilliant sketch of the young Indian guys 'going out for an English'. I was never fond of Indian cuisine until I went to Mumbai and had the real McCoy. Yet I knew about the pleasures of numerous Indian restaurants with evocative names, such as the Light of Bengal, one of Aberdeen's best curry houses, where chapattis, vindaloos, masalas, Kashmiri chickens, jalfrezi dishes, lime pickle and chutney were all enjoyed of an evening by my bank colleagues. I also recall Younger's Indian Pale Ale on tap in the Broch, never fully appreciating its provenance – originally it was brewed to supply thirsty squaddies out servicing the dusty outpost of the Empire.

As my knowledge grew I came to understand more about the extent to which India and China were the new economic powerhouses of the world. They call them the BRIC economies of Brazil, Russia, India and China. I learned that India was the world's largest democracy, that its economy was booming and that this young nation of over 1.1 billion was a ripe market for all manner of goods and services. An affluent and highly educated Indian middle class of nearly 400 million was demanding the quality of life enjoyed in the West.

Yet most British people travelling to work in India have little understanding or appreciation of the subcontinent's immense culture and history. All of its indigenous empires and dynasties have come and gone, although from the 16th century India was part of the great Mughal empire which forged the subcontinent's Islamic religious legacy. We might know about Akbar the Great, who represented the zenith of this empire in 1556; we might know that the British Raj, including what became Pakistan and Bangladesh, created huge wealth for Britain. Lord Curzon, a former Indian Viceroy, stated in 1901: 'As long as we rule India we are the greatest power in the world. If we lose it we shall drop straightaway to a third-rate power.'

A third-rate power or not, I'm glad that our multicultural nation, which now embraces people from all over the globe, has done a lot to throw off its old imperialist superiority. None of this really meant much to me though in the 2000s. The years of British rule were over a long time ago. From a Scottish point of view, the belief was that the things that were done in India were, by and large, positive. The British gave the subcontinent its solid administration, the railway network and a moderately liberal government which brought peace and prosperity to a very rebellious and warlike part of the globe. But there can be no denying that under the Raj Indians were treated like second-class citizens in their own land. I've never had any time for snobs. I'm very proud of my working-class roots in a fishing community where people are tough but fair. I was brought up with the view that we're all Jock Tamson's Bairns, and that if you were prepared to roll your sleeves up, work hard and play fair with people, then you deserved a chance.

Today India is a vibrant and exciting place where there

is a palpable sense of optimism. However, when I arrived there for the first time, I felt enormous sympathy for all those people I saw trying to pull themselves out of the mire of poverty. Mumbai is India's commercial and entertainment centre – a symbol of the prosperity of modern India – and before I went there, perhaps naively, I had little idea of the darker side. And of course I had absolutely no notion that the West's battle against the terrorists of al-Qaeda, the fighters of the Taleban and the group known as Lashkar-e-Taiba would impinge directly on my life.

I had been with RBS for 22 years when I took up a role in the new RBS World Headquarters in Gogarburn, on the outskirts of Edinburgh. And here I'd like to explain a little about my path, not out of vanity but mainly to give an impression of how I came to be in a position where I was going to India to work on a new venture.

I was accepted early on the bank's accelerated training scheme and, as already mentioned, after my time in Fraserburgh was moved to the Peterhead branch. Irene and I got married on 8 August 1987. After a reception in Banff Springs Hotel, we shot off to Tenerife on honeymoon, confetti in our hair – it was my first trip abroad. We made lots of friends in Peterhead. We both grew up a lot, taking on our responsibilities as members of the community and as parents of a young family. These were seven wonderful years. In 1993 I received my first managerial promotion and became responsible for a clutch of RBS branches in the North East.

Banking was changing. The Captain Mainwaring-type bank manager who knew all his customers personally, conducted business on the golf course, ate lots of lunches, and had real local autonomy was fast becoming a thing of the past. The new era was more about selling financial products such as insurance, mortgages and pensions. There was now a need for a sales force, which was something different for the bank. The whole concept of banks as sales outlets has been somewhat discredited by the banking collapse of 2008, but back in 1993 banking needed to strengthen its markets – and the public wanted it. It was a concept which was to place RBS in a position of strength in later years, enabling its takeover of the National Westminster Bank in 2000 to proceed so successfully.

The change of strategy required new skills and an increase in training for the staff. My first managerial post presented the ideal opportunity to move back to Macduff, where shortly after Stephanie was born I was promoted to Retail Manager, responsible for Aberdeen Queen's Cross (the North East flagship branch of RBS at the time) and Dyce. The daily commute from Macduff to Queen's Cross meant starting before 6am and returning home most nights after 8pm. This gave me little time with the family. To resolve this, we decided to move to Portlethen, just south of Aberdeen. We had only just unpacked our stuff from the flitting, when I was given responsibility for ten branches in the North East as opposed to Queen's Cross and Dyce.

I was now spending a great deal of my time on the road. It was fuzzy logic. Here I was driving on a daily basis from Portlethen, on the opposite side of Aberdeen, to where we had just moved from. I was looking after a gloriously scenic part of Scotland including Huntly, Dufftown, Keith, Banff, Peterhead, Alford, Inverurie, Turriff, and also Kirkwall in Orkney and Lerwick in Shetland – perhaps the largest single geographical footprint of any person working in the bank. On sparkling spring days it was a joy; during the long, cold, dark winters it could be a drudge.

Irene is an amazing woman: she understood the issues

of work, the miles of travel outwith office time, and my own expectations and commitment. She just got on with it, accepting that for me to move on within the bank meant frequent upheaval – and burning up a lot of miles on the road in my company car. She has always supported my career 100 per cent, so that when opportunities presented themselves those tough decisions were made so much easier.

For me, the essence of running a successful bank is having good people. You'd expect me to say this being someone who became increasingly involved in human resources. But good people need support: they require regular communication about what is happening and what is expected of them. They need to feel valued, included and part of the wider picture. They need nurture and supervision in equal measure. In October 1999, when I became a senior manager in RBS Retail Bank covering most of the north of Scotland, I was tasked with delivering the bank's strategy across seven regions for over 3,400 people, in what was known as the RICES programme.

It was important that the bank was not only able to recruit staff of the required calibre but also to ensure that we didn't lose good staff to our competitors. My team was constantly looking out for the right kind of people with the proper attitude to work in our branches. We delivered the induction training, supervised the sales roles to ensure they were properly conducted as per the regulations, and talent-spotted for the banking managers of the future.

When Irene and I moved back to Macduff, we had bought a new, four-bedroomed, detached house in Corskie Drive, but it wasn't ready so until it was we stayed with Irene's dad. As the new millennium approached we were excited about living in our new home.

I was engrossed in my job. I loved it. But now in role as a senior area manager covering the whole of Scotland, I spent more and more time away from home. In the six years prior to March 2006, a typical week had me waving goodbye early on a Monday morning, spending three nights in three different hotels and returning home very late on a Thursday. This was a sacrifice for the family that seemed to be essential if I was to move up in the bank. My commitment appeared to be paying off: in addition to the regular and healthy pay rises, I managed to win a number of top UK awards within the bank.

This did me a lot of favours and started to get me noticed externally, with a number of corporate 'head-hunters' trying to entice me into other organisations. My stock reply was: 'Thank you for thinking about me, but I'm happy with the Royal Bank of Scotland.'

I honestly didn't believe there was a better bank in the UK. For a while I was right. Each year, in an effort to highlight its growing global credentials, its best performers in the retail bank attended an annual conference overseas. I needed my passport – in 2002 I was winner of top area manager for HR in the UK at a conference in Rome; the following year, I was runner up for top area manager when we went to Barcelona, but regained the prize the following year in 2004 in New York, and topped this in 2005 when I won the Retail HR top performer at the Vienna conference. After this accolade, I remember a conversation with Irene, sitting around the kitchen table: we both knew my career had gone as far as it could if I remained based in the North East.

'There are new opportunities elsewhere, especially with expansion down in Edinburgh. What do you think I should do?'

'We all want you to do well, Roger,' Irene replied.
To progress further I would need to find a job in Edinburgh, where the Group's Human Resources team was based. This

was 150 miles from Macduff and would require a move. My discussion with Irene about the pros and cons of a move to Edinburgh was one that would shape our futures and set me on a path that culminated in my fateful visit to India.

RBS had achieved true global stature. The bank was Scotland's largest company by a mile – both in terms of stock market capital and the number of employees worldwide. As I've said, RBS had been able to take over the National Westminster Bank, a far larger bank, in a breath-taking piece of brinksmanship from the rival Bank of Scotland. RBS was so bullish it was able to take a full-page advert in the *Wall Street Journal* saying its market capital was greater than some famous brands such as Boeing and Coca Cola. Its annual report in 2002 showed that the Group's profit was £6.45 billion before tax and the share price was outstripping the FTSE 100 and Chairman Sir George Mathewson announced:

> In 2002 the Group continued to make good progress. The undoubted highlight was the completion of the NatWest IT integration on to the Royal Bank platform. This project – one of the largest integration projects ever undertaken worldwide – was completed ahead of schedule, with benefits well in excess of those promised to shareholders during the bid for NatWest.

The RBS board of directors included the great and the good of Scotland: Sir George Mathewson and Fred Goodwin at the helm; finance director Fred Watt; Sir Iain Vallance, vice-chairman and chairman of BT; Sir Angus Grossart, a doyenne of Scottish business life and chairman of Noble Grossart, the Edinburgh merchant bank; Bob Scott, former chief executive of insurance giant Norwich Union; Gordon Pell, formerly the managing director of Lloyds TSB Retail Banking, and two distinguished international executives, Lawrence Fish, the president and chief executive officer of Citizens Financial Group, in the United States, and non-executive Emilio Botin, the chairman of Banco Santander, one of Spain's biggest banks. Botin was an important friend and ally for RBS until Santander made its foray into the UK by buying Abbey National. In corporate banking, RBS now had added the clout of NatWest's global relationships and was able to undertake massive corporate deals and transformational financial activities around the globe, from the United States, Germany and Spain to Australia and Asia-Pacific. There were plans for new headquarters at Gogarburn, a custom-built base from which the bank would take forward its bold vision for developing its business internationally.

In what now seems like a golden age that will never return, there was a vim and vigour about the company which exhilarated me. While I loved living in Macduff with my family around me, I was ambitious to be at the hub contributing to the bank's expansion. As the bank's slogan had it, to 'Make It Happen'.

China and India were firmly on the horizon. In August 2005, RBS announced that it would lead a team, including a unit of Merrill Lynch and Hong Kong billionaire Li Ka-shing, in investing $3.1 billion to buy a 10 per cent stake in Bank of China. RBS was to put up $1.6 billion of its own cash. While investors were beginning to get a bit cagey about its global aspirations, the Bank of China deal would mean over 11,000 branches across a vast country of over one billion people. What opportunities lay ahead.

In July 2005 Sir Tom McKillop announced he was stepping down as chief executive of AstraZeneca, the pharmaceutical group, and was tipped to take over from Sir George Mathewson as chairman. At the time questions were raised in some quarters as to his suitability as chairman of a major bank, as he had no direct experience of financial services. Hindsight is a wonderful thing. With Sir George Mathewson gone, Fred continued with running the bank.

After looking after our children at home for 11 years, Irene had found a job she loved at Macduff Primary School, a few minutes' walk from our home. Lisa was heading to university in Aberdeen, while Christopher had taken on a four-year apprenticeship with a prominent building firm. All our friends and family were still living in and around the Macduff area. The decision was that if my career took me south, the family would stay put in Macduff.

And here a central part of my story comes into play. I had previously worked with Lynne Highway, who was now an important figure in HR in Gogarburn. So when the chance presented itself to join her team in Edinburgh, I promptly applied and successfully landed the job. I was to report for my new role in March 2006.

I would now be based in Edinburgh permanently with virtually no prospect of ever having a senior job within the RBS Group back in the North East. This meant that I was going to be with Irene and the kids only eight days a month, and during holidays. Doubts began to play in my head. Was I doing the right thing? What were my options? In my second week living in Edinburgh, sitting alone in my bedsit one evening, I was so homesick I started wondering what I was actually doing with my life and came within one phone call of reversing my decision.

But I knew in my heart that this was not an option. Over the years, when I've faced tough decisions I have remembered my brother who died so young and realised my own good fortune in having had the chance to make choices. Knowing that, I decided not to make the call, a decision that I know looking back was the right one.

The Royal Bank of Scotland's headquarters at Gogarburn, opened by the Queen in September 2005, is an impressive campus, reminiscent of an up-market, modern place of learning. It's a few minutes drive from the airport – handy for a bank with a global reach. The cluster of seven adjoining office buildings which accommodate over 3,200 bank employees is set in nearly 80 acres of grassy parkland dotted with mature trees; a brook runs through the grounds and there is a private golf course nearby.

Every visitor who comes through the revolving doors at the main entrance is greeted by two or three smartly-dressed security guards in dark blazers and must be signed in as a guest at the reception desk; the staff themselves have to flash their RBS photo-ID badges, which many wear on blue RBS-embossed lanyards around their necks. There is a constant flurry of activity in the entrance area, with people milling around awaiting colleagues or visitors, or rushing to catch the regular shuttle minibuses to the bank's other establishments in the city.

The front hallway is airy and spacious, reaching up to the height of three storeys to the glass roof which lets in shafts of bright daylight even on the dreichest Scottish autumn day. The acres of glass and the light sandstone finish on the concrete walls also create a very clean and crisp environment for work.

The whole reception area is almost like a covered village street, with a general store, a bookshop, an RBS branch, a chemist's, a fast-food sandwich outlet and a coffee stall. It is effectively the spine of the building, running its whole length, scattered with groups of chairs and tables; there is even a clump of trees six metres high. Along the left side are suites of meeting rooms. The finish is clean and comfortable, with grey granite tiles, and polished wooden stairs and landings.

The landings lead off to the numerous banking divisions or 'Houses', which look down onto the central 'street'. The building has taken a clutch of architectural prizes.

I worked in one of the open-plan offices – House A – set up for the Group's Human Resources; my desk was on the ground floor, alongside my colleagues in Policy & Advice, while Lynne Highway's glass-fronted office was one floor above. The gleaming corporate HQ, built on-time and on-budget, was a world-class place to work; the facilities, including the training rooms and education suites, were second to none. I knew myself fortunate to be among the cohort of over 3,250 staff welcomed to this new campus.

When I first arrived in Edinburgh, in March 2006, I was responsible for leading and managing a team of 30 HR professionals, as the Team Manager for Policy & Advice Services. We were at the end of a telephone providing advice on a range of employment law policies for line managers who were responsible for over 42,000 employees. I was tasked with motivating the team so that they delivered excellent customer service in an HR call-centre environment. I became involved with managing the relationship between the bank's specialist employment law centre, the HR Director for RBS Insurance and the managers within a division employing over 18,000 staff.

Then in 2007 RBS made a gigantic step: it led a consortium of Fortis Bank and Banco Santander to buy the Dutch bank ABN Amro, itself a giant global organisation. I vividly recall the period of the acquisition of ABN Amro, with RBS and Barclays battling it out for what was the coveted prize, and will never forget the positive feeling running right through RBS. You could almost touch it. We all had implicit faith in the executives, and Fred Goodwin (now Sir Fred), in particular. Despite adverse commentary in the press, we utterly believed that Sir Fred would land the deal of the decade and create a global platform for RBS to continue its unbelievable expansions in size, income and reputation. This was all a far cry from the company I had joined in the early 1990s, with its faltering share price and poor returns for investors.

The acquisition of ABN Amro, announced on 17 October 2007, was a watershed for the bank – and for so many of my colleagues at Gogarburn. We were riding the crest of a wave.

Throughout the months that were consumed by the bid, when RBS was battling with Barclays, the lunch-time chats in the corridor and in the 'street' were about our growing confidence that Sir Fred would once again deliver the goods. There was no anticipation whatsoever of an impending global financial collapse that would have so much impact on all of our lives. Our only trace of nervousness was the worry of what would happen if we didn't get ABN Amro and Barclays, our UK competitors, did.

The majority of staff in the Group had only ever been familiar with success: failure in any respect was never contemplated. While RBS could be a tough place to work, the leadership team had built a winning mentality comparable to that found within world-class sports teams: contemplating defeat was not an option. We had iconic golfer Jack Nicklaus, tennis star Andy Murray and three-times world racing car champion Sir Jackie Stewart as our sporting ambassadors. They exemplified the bank's winning mentality.

This pace and urgency were among the many exciting things about working for the organisation. Another benefit was the fact that its size meant you could have a varied career and change direction while remaining with the same employer, something that few organisations can offer. Following the ABN Amro deal, I was approached with a view to taking on a new role as the bank's Human Resources Global Project Implementation Manager. It was a grand title. It meant that I would be responsible for the design and implementation of a global HR service specialising in employment law and employee relations. I would head a small team managing a major change programme within Royal Bank of Scotland Human Resources. We would deliver a full review of the Group HR Operating Model, focusing on saving cost and eliminating duplication while maintaining efficiency and a fully compliant service. Lynne Highway called me upstairs to explain the details. I was immediately enthused. I relished working with uncertainty. I like it when I'm given a task with a wide remit and scope to be intuitive and creative. This hit all of those markers. I wanted the challenge. The initial weeks involved a lot of desk-based activity – research, making contacts and building networks in countries where I had no prior experience and knowledge. I was starting with a blank sheet of paper.

It was sometimes immensely frustrating. Fortunately I wasn't working in isolation here. The integration of a new business the size and magnitude of ABN Amro was massively complex. It required a lot of faith to drive forward into the unknown. Many senior managers and staff right across the banking group were now involved in landing their services in uncharted territory, right across the globe. We were now dealing with different languages, cultures, custom and practice, legal systems, and structures. This was complexity on the scale of a mission to the moon. For weeks I would arrive at my desk before 7am and often would be last out of the office in the evening. We were driven by the time differences between Edinburgh and India, which was five and a half hours ahead of us, or Asia-Pacific, which was nine hours ahead. There were audio conferences – other businesses call them conference calls – and meetings spanning several different time zones, with teams hooking up all over the place.

When I first joined Policy & Advice I had adopted an early-in, late-away work pattern and so I ploughed myself into this new challenge in similar style. It meant that I could get away sharp on Friday, across the Forth Road Bridge heading north, and be in Macduff for teatime with Irene and the family.

During the week I stayed with Euan Seatter, an old mate from Aberdeen and a fellow Dons fan, at his home in Dunfermline, just across the Forth Road Bridge in Fife, a quick commute to Gogarburn. We got on extremely well and spent our evenings either watching Champions League football on TV or battling it out with games of chess, where Euan tended to get the better of me. I was also a Liverpool fan, while he supported Manchester United, so there was the usual laddish banter about our teams' performances. We were both working hard, so we were in our beds early and away in the morning before the rush hour.

In my previous six-month project I had been responsible for the design and implementation of global HR services in this new era of employment law and employee relations. One specific job was to make it fit across 53 countries supporting the strategic aims of the growing Royal Bank. Banks are continually looking at ways of increasing their efficiency and stripping out unnecessary costs. My main responsibilities were to support a multi-million pound cost-savings target and manage a number of senior stakeholders to deliver this.

My key tasks included undertaking feasibility studies in a number of countries, designing human resources structures within strict budgets, and recruiting and training HR advisers and consultants. At the core, this sort of work is about people's lives and livelihoods and it requires a huge amount of sensitivity. It's not quite a science, but there are certainly ways of doing things properly – or getting it wrong. It was all very important for the bank and our big boss – Neil Roden, the Group HR Director – that we got this right. One part of my job was setting a course for employment while taking into account all the different legislation and cultures. This was especially relevant in my work in Mumbai.

For my first trip to Mumbai I attended to all of the travel arrangements and collected my visa, arranged my airport pick-up at the other side and times of the meetings with key staff.

As well as managing my project, I was the only person from Policy & Advice so the support I had in setting up the systems and integrating the technology was from an Australian called Carolyn Chan, an IT expert on a short-term contract with RBS. She actually lived in Australia, but had moved temporarily to Mumbai to set up our IT system. She was brilliant and had gathered a small team that I got to know really well during my first visit. Our two support staff were Indian nationals and the work and service from them was excellent.

On Sunday 28 September I flew from Dyce to Heathrow and then from Heathrow to Mumbai, where we touched down at around 11am on Monday 29 September. I got up at 4:30 the next morning to fly to Delhi where I spent the day cocooned in a meeting room delivering a presentation to a large group of senior heads with whom I debated at length the funding and resources needed for this new service. I used every available minute, only leaving when to have stayed a moment longer would have meant missing my return flight to Mumbai. A taxi miraculously negotiated the chaotic traffic and got me back to the airport in time. I got back to the Oberoi just before midnight at the end of an exhausting day.

Wednesday and Thursday were spent mainly in back-to-back sessions in windowless rooms, interviewing or poring over piles of paperwork. I could have been anywhere in the world – until I emerged into the dusky evening and the unmistakable sights and sounds of Mumbai.

CHAPTER FIVE

Return to India

THE DAY OF my second trip to India was Sunday 23 November 2008. I got up and pulled open the curtains to find it had been snowing heavily and the whole scene outside our Macduff home looked like a Victorian Christmas card. It was minus 4 degrees – but I soon warmed up digging the car out and clearing the driveway. I needed to make the, usually, 40-minute journey to Aberdeen Airport in Dyce later in the afternoon. Otherwise it was a normal family Sunday, except that instead of having our meal at about 5pm, joined by Irene's dad, today we sat down to eat the roast at noon.

Having been out to Mumbai only seven weeks earlier, I knew the ropes and wasn't unduly concerned about the logistics of this trip. I already held a three-month visa. This second trip was originally booked for the following week, but I had found out that it coincided with a huge festival which would possibly disrupt my programme of meetings and so we had rescheduled.

There were just so many coincidences as to why I ended up in the middle of the attacks – a little like my brother, who was not meant to be aboard the *Bon Ami* on the day he lost his life, having swapped berths with the skipper's son. Last time at the Oberoi I had stayed on the 15th floor – exactly where the terrorists were to be during their final gun battles with the Indian Army. This time I had a room on the 14th floor.

I had packed my clothes, including a dark-blue RBS suit, designed by Jeff Banks, and compulsory RBS necktie with its red and gold motif. Even although I was heading to India on business, the idea of going to this amazing country still felt very exotic to me, and I was looking forward to it. I expected to be back home the following Friday, safe and sound. Air travel on modern planes run by European and American airlines is one of the safest forms of transport. I'm like any other traveller when it gets bumpy or there is air turbulence, but generally I love the experience.

After lunch we all helped clear the table – as usual the family dynamic was very good-natured and we had some laughs together. Then I said goodbye to Irene and the kids and set off for Dyce with the roads pretty clear. At Aberdeen airport I left the car in the long-stay car park and headed into the terminal, which was gratifyingly warm and remarkably busy for a winter Sunday. There were queues at the check-in desks because of a fault with the conveyor belt which takes the baggage through to the airside dispatch area, so I had to check in at a different area before making my way through to the departure lounge. Travelling business class with British Airways has its perks. I settled down to a coffee and a read of the Sunday newspapers. Then it was announced that my flight to Heathrow was delayed.

Apparently the in-bound flight had been affected by a rumpus, four passengers being escorted off the plane for drinking too much. I scanned my fellow passengers in the executive departure lounge. A Malaysian woman and her daughter sitting in the row in front of me looked to be leaving Scotland for a long time – or even for good. I concluded that she must be an ex-employee of the airport because a gentleman working in the lounge handed her a gift and they spent a lot of time chatting before he took his leave, wishing her well. Then, looking around, I recognised a familiar television celebrity with his partner making his way back to London – it was a dandy Englishman from a BBC makeover show, flamboyantly dressed in a leather trench coat. The cuffs and collar on his shirt were huge. But I couldn't think what his name was. I texted Stephanie. She would know.

Steph, who's the posh guy from Changing Rooms?

Quick as a flash my Blackberry bleeped.

Is it Laurence Llewelyn-Bowen?

That's him. He's in the lounge. I knew you'd know. Love dad.

I sat watching the television news and then Irene called. She was concerned because Christopher had lost his mobile phone the previous night – he'd left it in the taxi he'd taken home – and I had to arrange to cancel it and make sure the SIM card was blocked so that no one else could use it.

The flight eventually took off and we made it to Heathrow an hour and a half later. I was glad to stretch my legs as I headed over to the international departure terminal and wandered around one or two of the shops. I browsed at the duty-free and found that I was peckish again. I have this sneaking suspicion that the airlines are in cahoots with the retail outlets and that we spend more time in the departure area than is really necessary. My flight to Mumbai was due to depart from Gate 42 at 10.30pm. I was in need of another sandwich.

The irony of travelling business class to India is that you can get a wonderful selection of food on board as part of the premium service, but if you've been travelling all day, it's rather too late. I thought it was better to grab a cheese and tomato toastie in one of the kiosks, and pass on the possibility of in-flight smoked salmon and caviar: better use the flight time to sleep. The following day I would have a lengthy taxi journey into Mumbai and then have to get straight down to work.

I continued my people-watching. There were a few Indian nationals waiting to board, and I tried to work out what they did and what sort of backgrounds they came from. A BA Business Class flight from London to Mumbai costs several thousand pounds – the equivalent of almost a year's wages for many of the Indian executives that I would be meeting. I imagined that those people in the lounge must have done incredibly well from India's booming economy, the successful few against the backdrop of over a billion people, many of whom find keeping body and soul together problematic.

When the flight was called I was directed to a short queue in a cordoned-off area for First and Business Class travellers. Some of the passengers in the longer Economy Class queue craned their necks to see who was stepping forward – and I joked to myself that they would be disappointed if they were hoping to see a Bollywood star or a Maharajah.

On boarding, I made myself comfortable in my own 'pod', a seat which turns into a full-length bed. This was only the second time that I'd gone Business Class. It certainly is a comfortable way to travel. The air steward offered me a choice of Champagne or freshly-squeezed orange juice. I'm not a lover of Champagne, so I plumped for the orange. I used to find water boring to drink – but my perspective on this would change radically by the end of this week. I only glanced at the menu, but didn't give in to the temptations there. I removed the blue blanket from its plastic bag and put the earphones for the television and radio into the small drawer that pulled out at my feet. Despite the engine noise and occasional turbulence, I soon dropped off to sleep.

At 5am I was awakened unceremoniously when the footstool which made up the lower half of the bed snapped away from its supporting bracket in the seat. The noise of the crash brought over the stewardess. She tried to sort it but eventually had to concede that it was well and truly broken.

I was prepared for the meetings ahead, but decided to read through my notes and check the material for the rest of the week as I munched on a breakfast of orange juice and croissants; I also wanted to think over what was on the agenda for my major meetings in the ABN Amro building, which was just around the corner from the Oberoi Hotel.

Eventually we swept in over Mumbai. I peered out of the window to see that the sun had risen on a wonderful clear day. The scene below looked strikingly different from the snow-covered North East of Scotland. As we descended I could clearly see the shanty towns where literally millions of people lived in poverty.

The plane touched down at 11.50am local time.

To say the Chattrapathi Shivaji International Airport is busy is an understatement and it took a while to get through the necessary controls. I've always had a reasonably good sense of direction, so I wasn't thrown by the general sense of chaos and I felt calm as I picked up my bags and left the terminal. Outside it was like standing in front of an open blast-furnace door. I found myself in the middle of a huge surge of people, many searching for friends, relations or acquaintances, some holding up signs with names scrawled on them. This was India.

As I scanned the crowd, I was relieved to spot a white-suited man dressed in what I recognised to be the livery of the Oberoi Hotel; he was waving his peaked cap and holding up a sign for 'Mr Hunt'. I wove my way towards him through the crowd. He smiled, introduced himself as Bharat and said, 'Welcome to India,' then took my suitcase.

The broiling mid-day heat was overwhelming and I was soaked with sweat within a few steps of the terminal door. As Bharat led me over what appeared to be some waste ground – the airport car park – I was astonished to see a little girl and her small brother, both of whom I recognised from my previous trip. As before they were begging.

Seeing this slip of a girl emerge from between some parked cars immediately took me back to my previous trip. She was wearing the same ill-fitting frock and looked very unkempt; there was dirt ingrained under her fingernails and her hair was matted. But there was no shame in her manner as she dogged my steps, tugging at my sleeve and gesturing at her mouth to show me she wanted food. The little boy was about five years old, a picture of innocence. He was wearing shorts and had a T-shirt draped over his shoulders to stop the sun burning him. He walked a few paces behind the girl, watching like an attentive apprentice learning a trade. He backed off when the driver gestured at them, whereas the girl was resolute, although not at all offensive.

I couldn't avoid the possibility that this might be her only chance to secure something to eat or drink that day. They had probably been out in the scorching heat all morning and looked very dry and tired. What an existence. It seemed exraordinary that I should actually recognise them, given all the people milling around; but then, this was to be no ordinary trip.

Bharat opened the door of the Mercedes for me and I sat in the back seat. I knew from my previous trip that there would be a couple of bottles of cool water and a cold facecloth in the car. While Bharat was putting my luggage into the boot I picked up the bottles.

Bharat anticipated my intention.

'Please, sir, don't do this,' he said.

I looked at him with a puzzled expression. I had a bottle in each hand and the two street children were right there outside the car. I was filled with sympathy for them and couldn't help thinking of my own kids back in Scotland and so I ignored him and handed each child a bottle of water.

Bharat chased off the scruffy pair, who were now grinning from ear to ear, and then softly scolded me:

'You shouldn't do this, sir, it will only encourage them.'

I felt so sorry for these kids. Had this episode been in the streets of Aberdeen, a prosperous oil and gas industry city in Scotland, the whole incident would have provoked a gruffer response from me. I vowed that on my proposed return to Mumbai in early 2009 I would give them something if they were still begging in the dusty car park, regardless of the advice of my driver.

I knew that the trip to the hotel would be rather harrowing. I was conscious of sitting in a chauffeur-driven, air-conditioned Merc speeding past the shanty towns and dormitory villages that lined the motorway. All along the route people were conducting their lives out in the open: cooking food; sleeping on mats; playing card games. Children scampered about in drains and over dusty wastelands. They often tried to attract our attention.

There seemed no rhyme or reason to the road system. Bharat was an excellent driver and had the advantage of a powerful, properly serviced vehicle, which powered through a chaos of motorbikes, 'tuk-tuk' motorcycle taxis, mopeds, pedal bicycles, packed buses, trucks belching clouds of carbon, battered black and yellow taxis, and the ubiquitous Morris Ambassador saloon cars.

Every time we stopped at a red light or were held up by a vehicle in front, a woman with a baby in her arms would approach and tap on the window. The babies were dressed in little more than a dirty rag tied around them and looked as if they hadn't been fed for some time. Although my heart went out to these people and it made me appreciate what I had in Scotland, I knew that there was little I could do. If I asked Bharat to roll down the window, we would have been mobbed. The best thing was to turn my attention away as best I could. This felt wrong but it was really the only course of action. I reminded myself that I was in India to help bring high quality jobs to the country; surely that was what I could do to enable more people to be pulled out of the poverty trap.

To occupy my mind and blot out some of the worst aspects of the journey, I started asking Bharat about himself. He was a friendly guy who took an interest in his passengers. He told me that he had a young family. He'd been driving for the Oberoi Hotel for five years and was very experienced in dealing with the city.

'Where are you from, sir?' he asked.

'I'm from Scotland,' I replied.

'Where is that?'

'It's in the UK.'

'I'm sorry, I don't know "UK".'

'Have you heard of London?'

'Yes, yes. London is a big city, like Mumbai.'

'Well, London is the big city in the UK and Scotland is a part of that country too.'

'Oh, I see,' he replied. But I was sure he didn't.

'London is very rich place, I hear,' Bharat said.

'I think it is.'

'So how much would this fine car be in the UK?'

'Probably about £50,000.'

'How many rupees is that?'

'I'm not so sure – but it would probably be the equivalent of many people's yearly income in Mumbai,' I said.

I realised that Scotland was an incredibly small country in global terms – and that billions of people will never have heard of it, never mind knowing about the charms of a place like Macduff!

Bharat eagerly pointed out some of the landmarks of his amazing city. He was especially proud of the cricket grounds, the Bombay Oval. Everywhere there were kids with bats and balls, and I could see dozens of games going on in the streets and behind the high fences in the green, watered lawns of the elite clubs. India is the world's number one cricket nation and it's obvious even to the casual visitor with little interest in the game that it is a huge part of life. While many people have very little, the sport represents their dreams and aspirations.

CHAPTER SIX

A Grand Arrival

AS WE HIT the city centre the traffic became even more congested. Making progress now was difficult. We drove forward only a few feet at a time, frequently braking to an abrupt halt. The noisy, dusty road was like a supercharged starting grid where all kinds of vehicles were pushing for position. When we stopped, young boys, many with limbs missing, would come and knock on the window looking for money and drinks. I had tried to ignore this welter of humanity, but it was such an extraordinary scene. There were children being bathed in the street; cattle wandering down the road; such in-your-face poverty that it was impossible not to be affected by it all. I thought about the massive chasm between people's lives in the UK and those in India for whom it was all about survival.

My destination was, by contrast, one of the most luxurious places you could hope to stay. The Oberoi, part of a top notch Indian chain, is one of the best hotels in the world. The bank's local agents had recommended it because of its convenient location, a street away from the ABN Amro building where I would be working for the first two days of my stay. I had considered booking another hotel which was recommended by a bank colleague and was nearer to Mafatlal Mills, where I would be working for the remainder of the week, but I plumped for the Oberoi. It would be simple to take a taxi to the Mafatlal Mills. I'd bumped into three RBS employees getting off the British Airways flight in Mumbai and learned that they were all staying on the opposite side of the city. Had I joined them, I would have been entirely clear of the events of 26 November.

Our Mercedes approached the Oberoi along the Queen's Necklace, an ocean-side stretch which reminded me of Aberdeen's Beach Boulevard, only the sea was sparkling aquamarine in the sunshine. Bharat steered the car right to the hotel front door underneath the glass canopy.

There was a line of pristine Mercedes with chauffeurs in white suits, the head concierge wearing an immaculate white turban, and younger assistants waiting to greet me and take my bags. On my previous visit, the driver had insisted that I stayed seated to allow him to open the door, because his every action was on show and any perceived shortfall in his service could mean him losing his job. So I waited until Bharat opened the door before I stepped out of the Merc and the mid-day heat once again blasted me.

'Good day, sir. Welcome to the Oberoi. We hope you enjoy your stay. Can I take you up to the first floor check-in?' said the head concierge.

I nodded and followed him through the gleaming glass door, past a security guard and through a metallic door-framed detector, then headed up a flight of stairs to the main lobby. The check-in area was in a massive modern atrium with a polished red marble tiled-floor, fuchsia and mauve Persian rugs and ornate chandeliers. Water bubbled in the fountain. I'd stayed in a number of lovely international hotels, but one aspect which I found particularly pleasing here was the height and vastness of the lobby. As I stood waiting for the receptionist to take my details, I gazed around. It was like a magnificent palace. There was the grand piano, sumptuous grey leather sofas and green foliage streaming down from each balcony. I remembered the relaxed café off to the left where they served savouries and coffee, and straight across the lobby, which seemed like a football pitch away, was the Tiffin Restaurant. I'd thoroughly enjoyed dining there before, and I was looking forward to my next visit.

On the first floor there was the Kandahar restaurant where I had savoured real Indian cuisine. My whole family loves Indian meals back in Scotland. Chicken tikkas, masalas, rogan joshes, vindaloos, I thought I knew about them all, but I have to confess I'd never really enjoyed them all that much. Then, on my previous visit to Mumbai, a waiter called Maclean had looked after me as I dined in the Kandahar. I was intrigued by his name, which sounded so Scottish, so I asked him about it. He told me he had started calling himself Maclean after seeing Bruce Willis in one of the *Die Hard* films. This made me laugh. And I liked his style. He very sensitively encouraged me to sample the north-west Indian cuisine on offer there and the sweet malpua pancakes with nuts were a revelation to my taste buds.

From the check-in you could look through to the shopping mall, where luxury designer brands like Armani, Gucci and Mulberry had emporiums. The mall led through to the Oberoi's sister hotel, the Trident.

I was given my keys to Room 1478 and escorted there by a well-dressed young Indian woman. The door to the room was made of heavy, dark wood and it opened onto a short, narrow lobby. She led me further into my room and made sure I had some water. A porter arrived with my case and then an older woman, elegant and with a rather superior air, also came in. She handed me an embossed card, which introduced her as Georgette Hegde, 'Butler'. She told me she would be on call during my stay and that if I needed anything I was to ask her staff. They were all most courteous and pleasantly helpful. I was astonished that there were three hotel staff in the room at the one time. Where else in the world was a visitor likely to get this level of attention? I gave them all a tip and they disappeared quickly to give me some space.

After my hours of travel I was at last alone. I decided to try and open the window and get my bearings but it was tightly shut, presumably a safety feature. I noticed that this room was identical to the one I'd occupied on the floor above.

Through a louvred door on the right was a carpeted dressing room in which a low storage unit of polished oak ran the whole length of the left wall. It contained a safe. Above the unit was a huge mirror. Against the right wall stood a fitted wardrobe with two tall sliding doors, with a small split cupboard on top for storing T-shirts etc. Straight ahead was a double vanity unit with two wash-hand basins and gold-plated taps. Above both basins was another huge mirror and a suspended wire tray with a collection of shampoos, moisturizer, shower gels, a shoe-horn and a comb. I opened a door to reveal a sunken bath and an open-plan shower, which looked most inviting after my clammy journey. Straight ahead in white enamel porcelain was a water closet and a bidet.

The main bedroom was approximately 14ft by 14ft, bigger then the main bedroom in a modern newly-built home in the UK. It was fully carpeted with a freshly-painted cream and brown colour scheme. On the left wall was the cabinet which held the minibar and the fridge; on top of it sat a slim black television.

In the far left-hand corner was a solid writing bureau which was where I worked late into the evening, writing up my notes and preparing for the following day. The drawer contained brochures about Mumbai and the hotel itself, a smart notepad and some black Oberoi pens. Beside the 'executive' seat was a small table bearing a lamp, a plate full of juicy plums which looked as though they had been polished, and a small silver-plated knife.

The bed stood on the right, flanked by a couple of small bedside tables, one containing the room phone. Above the bed, which was boxed into the floor, was a set of angle-poise lights which could be switched on from either side of it. The fluffy pillows were absolutely huge – they virtually wrapped themselves around your head.

A two-seater sofa was placed square on to the far right wall and in front of it was a glass-topped coffee table. The huge window, which ran the full length of the wall opposite the door, had a thin mosquito screen and a set of heavy curtains which dropped all the way to the floor.

I switched on the television and watched the hotel's welcome message, then phoned reception and asked for an iron and an ironing board, because my clothes had become creased and crumpled after their trip.

Within about 20 minutes I'd showered, shaved and put on my suit and freshly ironed shirt. I got some Indian currency and then skipped down the steps and out into the sunshine. I headed round the back of the hotel to the ABN Amro building at Sakhar Bhavan, on Nariman Point, to meet some of the colleagues who had been working on the integration programme with me, including Kate Averre, the manager for the HR integration in India. She had only been on the project for about six weeks but during that period, through numerous conversations on audio conference and one-to-one calls, I had struck up a good working relationship with her. Her husband, Nick, was also in town, over from Jersey for a week's sightseeing. I was keen to meet Kate in person.

I went into the modern ABN Amro office block, which stands opposite the British Council. Inside the lift there was a young man ready to push the buttons for the requisite floor. This used to be commonplace in certain department stores in Edinburgh and London, but the practice has virtually disappeared in the UK. Anyway, I was reminded of that corny old Bob Hope joke – a job as a bell-hop has its ups and downs.

At the floor for HR I was met by a security guard and taken through to greet Kate. She in turn introduced me to the rest of the team. These were to be our new colleagues and part of our integration of ABN Amro with Royal Bank.

'Pleased to meet you in person,' said Kate.

'I'm delighted to be here again,' I said.

'Did you have a good trip?' inquired another colleague.

'Excellent.'

'Would you like some tea?

'I'd love a cup.'

Normally I take it in turns with colleagues to make the tea, dunking in a teabag, a splash of semi-skimmed milk from the carton, and offering a quick cup to anyone else in the vicinity who fancies a hot drink. So I was fully prepared to make my own. But a man approached and shook his finger at me. Tea-making was his job – and he took it seriously.

The team sat down around a table and began chatting. There was also a tempting bowl of tropical fruit, including mangoes and bananas and as I lent forward to dip my hand in, the smiling man approached again.

'Let me take that for you, sir.'

He took the fruit out of my hand and disappeared into a kitchen area, emerging moments later with a beautifully cut fruit cocktail, which I munched at as we all got to know each other.

This tiny episode with the 'tea wallah' made me think about the importance of everyone's job. In the UK, efficiencies in the banking industry had been driven by getting rid of superfluous jobs and duplication. My remit had been to identify such efficiencies, but here I was getting a lesson first-hand on the importance of keeping people in gainful work; while a man serving tea might appear a luxury in a European setting, in India the employment situation and the implications of being jobless were quite different. To be in employment and have a regular income, however modest, was no doubt a real achievement in this context.

We completed our work quickly. I heard about the progress being made and I was heartened to learn that so much was already in place for our main meetings on Wednesday. I also met one of my senior colleagues, Gavin Reid, who would become a lifeline for me in the days to follow. Gavin, a fellow Scot from Kintyre and now head of RBS's change programmes, had been based in Mumbai for six months and was already immersed in the city's vibrant culture. He was keen to show me around and apologised that he wouldn't be able to meet me for dinner later that evening. However, he promised that something would be arranged during the week.

My preference was for a light supper in the hotel, an evening saunter out along the Queen's Necklace, and a late-night call to Irene. Little did I know there would be another escapade to write home about.

CHAPTER SEVEN

An Indian Wedding

FOREIGN TRAVEL ACROSS time zones can upset your routines. It plays havoc with your natural body clock and sleep patterns and disrupts when you feel hungry enough to eat. I had been in Mumbai all day, spending the afternoon in the office. I'd eaten nothing apart from the fruit cocktail, but I wasn't hungry.

I finished work at 5.30pm on Monday evening, well satisfied with what we had achieved. I walked back to the Oberoi in the stultifying heat, dropped into the café area for a cold drink before browsing around the designer shops looking for some scarves for Lisa and Stephanie. The air-conditioned mall was very cool and enticing; however I was cautious not to appear too keen to buy. On my previous visit an over-zealous shop assistant had phoned me in my hotel room and wanted to meet me in the foyer to conclude a sale – and I had thought this was just too pushy, and a surprising approach from such an up-market retailer.

I went up to my room, showered and returned to the Tiffin for supper. The hotel was now a lot busier. There was soothing live music in the foyer, where a pianist was deftly tinkling the ivories accompanied by some silky violinists and a harp player. It was all pleasant and calming.

After supper I returned to my room, ironed my shirts for the rest of the week, charged my Blackberry and my office and personal phones, then decided to go for an evening saunter. It had become a ritual for me last time – wandering along the Queen's Necklace, with its fantastic views of the Mumbai skyline and the bay. On my stroll I was mesmerised by the vitality of Indian life and the throngs of people enjoying the last of the evening sunshine. It was still very warm but, at last, there was a gentle breeze wafting in from the Arabian Sea. I noticed the blue RBS logo on one of the high-rise office blocks, and I felt a twinge of pride that this Scottish company now had such a global footprint.

I had a bottle of Himalayan branded water with me and this time I ventured much further than on my previous trip. It was one of those 'glad-to-be-alive' moments; the upbeat atmosphere of Mumbai was brilliantly infectious. Yes, there were sad sights, beggars and disabled people, but the overall atmosphere uplifted the spirit. I strode along at a fair pace, feeling safe although aware that there were now very few tourists around; the further I ventured from the Oberoi, the more unusual I must have appeared: a 5ft 8in, slim-built, casually-dressed white Westerner marching out along the promenade. I was aware of people staring – one or two even came up and touched me, then went off again.

I had been walking for over half an hour and it was growing darker. The sunset was a golden haze as the fiery sun began to disappear under the horizon of the shimmering sea. At a road junction I spotted some brightly-lit buildings painted in vivid red, tangerine, yellow and blue, and festooned with flowers and plants. I had never before seen such an amazingly vibrant building. It was almost like an Indian fairground attraction with hundreds of fairy lights, so unusual and pretty that I decided to cross the dual carriageway to investigate and capture the scene in a photo. It took ages to negotiate the traffic. As I got nearer, I switched on my compact digital camera. I could now see that the buildings were temporary structures, more like a staging for a film set; merely the enticing frontages. I thought that I might have stumbled upon a famous Bollywood film set. That only made me more curious. There was an exquisite display of lilies, carnations, roses and hibiscus, amber, white and purple; a scarlet carpet adorned a staircase that led up to a gold-painted double doorway. This was an ostentatious showcase.

As I was about to take a picture, a stocky Indian with a neat beard stepped forward. He didn't look too enamoured with me and I thought this was a security guard who was going to grab my camera and send me on my way. But instead of a reprimand, he placed his arm on my shoulder and then beckoned me towards the golden doorway.

'What is happening?' I asked, thinking it might be some kind of illicit gaming establishment.

'It's a wedding, sahib. Please, come in.'

'I couldn't possibly go to a wedding I haven't been invited to.'

'Well, you're invited now.' he replied.

I thought: *I'm Scottish – I can't just gatecrash some strangers' wedding.* But the guy was adamant. I climbed the steps and went through the golden doors. It was like stepping through the wardrobe in *The Lion, the Witch and the Wardrobe*. Here was another magical world, lit by strings of hundreds of fairy-lights. Tables covered in glistening white silk were covered with a display of delicately wrapped wedding presents. It somehow reminded me of the final moments of the old television show, *The Generation Game*, when all the prizes were laid out for the winner.

I could now see that there was a spacious, well-tended garden area behind the facade. About a hundred metres away white awnings framed a small stage on which stood two thrones covered with red velvet cushions; a couch stood on either side of the throne. There were also rows upon rows of seats, each with white cotton covers. This was obviously where the wedding service had taken place. The noise of laughter, clinking glasses and crockery was coming from a tented area out of which children were spilling to run around the garden.

I was taking a few pictures of the wedding presents when I was approached by a group of young, immaculately dressed Indians who seemed genuinely delighted that I was snapping their event. Although, they were smiling I eased my way back to the door, so as not to intrude any further. Then another couple marched up to me.

'Would you like to take our pictures?' inquired the man.

'Yes, I'd like that,' I laughed.

The women all looked fantastic in their flowing sarees; the guys were equally resplendent, some wearing silk turbans with emeralds on the front.

I had just about got everyone into the picture when, 'Hold on please, hold on,' cried one of the girls and ran out of view and down the stairs. Seconds later she ran back into viewfinder range, pulling someone by the hand. It was the bride. She wore an ornate saree of richly embroidered pink and saffron silk encrusted with jewels, and a traditional *gajra* – a floral trail – which was clipped to her hair and dropped down to her waist. Her hands were painted in elaborate henna designs and her face was beautifully made-up; she had a bejewelled ring punched through her nostril, an ostentatious necklace of ruby-red stones, and a cluster of silver and amber bangles around each wrist. I felt rather in awe; she appeared so serene and regal, exacly as I imagined a maharajah's daughter.

She took her position in the centre of the group and her friends giggled loudly as I clicked away. Then the bride held her hand over her mouth and whispered to one of her friends, who translated for me:

'She says that it is good luck to have a tall stranger at a wedding. You are a good luck charm.'

I laughed at that – and everyone else joined in. It was a moment of shared joy and common humanity, across very different cultures.

I wished her good luck and kind greetings to her and her new husband from this stranger from Scotland, and as this was translated back to her she looked delighted. It was time to head back to the hotel. I waved goodbye and began my trek back, still amused to have been part of a wedding of people I'd never met before.

An hour later I was in my room, feet up on the bed, head resting on the voluminous pillows, and chatting to Irene in Macduff. I warned her I had another tale to tell and recounted my wedding story. I could hear her laughing – 'Typical Roger, you've aye got a story to tell,' she joked.

The next day was going to be full-on. I went down to breakfast in the Tiffin restaurant and on the way I picked up a copy of *The Times of India* to read some local news. Although it was early, there was quite a lot of American voices around a cluster of tables. They were noisy and exuberant, in a very nice kind of way. One figure stood out among this gregarious band of folk: a tall, slimly built, rather teacherly American with big glasses and a gentle face. I later learned this was Alan Scherr, a 58-year-old from Virginia, who had with him his only child, his 13-year-old daughter, Naomi. Their party was on a spiritual pilgrimage. Predominantly they were a middle-aged group, including four Canadians, an Australian and about 16 Americans; one or two had walking sticks but most were fit-looking. They appeared a contented and close-knit bunch. Alan was very ready to joke and laugh but there was a calmness and serenity about him that I admired.

I made solid progress at work, pushing on through lunch and finishing about 4pm, so I headed back to the hotel. Tomorrow I would be moving up to Mafatlal Mills for the next round of meetings, so I decided to sit outside by the swimming pool, read my notes and answer emails. I changed into shorts and a T-shirt and found a sun-recliner in the shade with a stunning view overlooking the shimmering Arabian Sea. Guests could see out over the bay, but people walking along the Queen's Necklace couldn't see in because the small pool was secluded and above road level. It was a very comfortable sun-bed with padded cushions, and I draped my thick white cotton towel over the back. The sky was azure. One of the waiters approached and placed a delicate tray of fruit kebabs on the table beside me. He then handed me a package of sun-block cream and a face-cloth. I asked for a soft drink and within moments a large, cool juice arrived packed with crushed ice and topped with a slice of lemon. I thought how surreal this was: sitting in a classy hotel in India and working for one of the world's best banks. But I was temporarily startled as a crow flapped onto a nearby table and snapped up a segment of pineapple. What a fearless scavenger! It obviously knew there were rich pickings in this place.

There was no one else in the pool area until a couple of Western women arrived: one a young blonde-haired teenager; the other a woman who could have been her mother, but whose demeanour indicated to me that she was more a family friend. I smiled as they passed, and the older woman nodded back. They pulled off their robes and jumped into the pool. For the next 15 minutes or so they splashed around laughing and shouting playfully, taking turns to chase and then soak each other. The sight of their carefree frolicking raised my spirits after my concentrated day's work. As I headed to my room I detoured briefly across to the poolside to warn them to watch out for cheeky crows ready to pinch their fruit kebabs. They both laughed and thanked me for my warning. I later learned the teenager was Naomi Scherr.

That evening I caught up with Gavin and we dined at the Taj Mahal Palace & Tower Hotel with Kate and Nick. This hotel is a landmark for the city, just minutes from the Gateway of India monument, and overlooking the Arabian Sea. The reception was thronged with guests and attentive staff in traditional Indian garb. The restaurant was outstanding: one of the best places I have ever eaten. The rule was no office talk this evening, so we listened to Nick's tales of visiting a mosque and his trip to an Indian tiger village. The food was a feast for the senses and it was plain why this place had a reputation for being among the finest hotels in the world. It was another great experience for me and I returned to the Oberoi thoroughly enchanted by the wonderful city of Mumbai.

CHAPTER EIGHT

Lifesaving Birthday Cake

I WAS ALREADY awake when my travel alarm clock rasped into life at 6am on Wednesday 26 November. I had woken up with the light of dawn seeping into my room. As I lay for a few minutes surfacing, I reflected that I had only been in Mumbai two days, but what a fantastic time I'd had. I smiled at the thought of being a good luck charm at the wedding.

Today I was looking forward to being able to make an announcement about new jobs in India. Today was special: the culmination of many weeks of planning, thinking, meetings and hard work. This would create a lot of personal excitement for many individuals. And I was getting the opportunity to train people, using the material I had prepared back in Britain.

I got up, showered, dressed and headed down for breakfast in the Tiffin. In the lobby that morning were the now-familiar American visitors. The tall American was again going around the group saying good morning and dispensing laughter and jokes.

I was keen to get going. After all, this was my reason for being in India. It was why I was picking up a monthly salary from the Royal Bank of Scotland. I didn't want to tarry too long in the hotel and I'd arranged for Bharat to collect me at 7.30. I was heading out to Mafatlal Mills for the whole day with Sean Rodriquez, a colleague who had worked in

Policy & Advice in Gogarburn with me. He had kicked off his career in Edinburgh but he would now be managing the team in India – having worked in Delhi, he had now settled in Mumbai.

I got into the lift with one of the American party, the woman I had seen in the swimming pool the previous evening. We exchanged pleasantries and I asked her if she was on holiday.

'Not exactly,' she replied. 'We're over from the States on a meditation week. It's been a very good time. We're heading back home on Monday.'

I thought I detected an Irish lilt in her American drawl.

She inquired about my work and where I was from – and then the lift opened at the 12th floor, and she got out. Just another tiny human encounter that I would recall many days later.

I met Bharat outside the front of the hotel. As usual, he was immaculately dressed and gave me a warm greeting and a huge smile.

'Good morning, sir,' he said. 'Perhaps you'd like to read the morning paper.'

He handed me a copy of *The Times of India*, which I was beginning to enjoy, a bottle of water and a cold facecloth.

'How long will the journey take?' I asked.

'I think it will take about an hour – but it depends on the traffic. The radio reports that it's pretty busy again this morning.'

We set off across the Beach Front, along Marine Drive, around the Queen's Necklace and reached the first major junction where we slowed to join the traffic at Chowpatty. Already at this early hour, a barefooted mother holding a baby in her arms approached and gawped in the window at me. The child was crying so hard its eyes were red-raw. The mother looked so forlorn as she made the typical gesture, fingers closed together, putting her hand up to her mouth. Such moments were once more a regular feature of the journey across the city. There were children playing on the road, right in among the cars and streams of people heading for a day at the race course. Destitute people were raking in garbage for anything that could be recycled. It all felt unreal after the palatial opulence of the Oberoi and I experienced an overwhelming sense of guilt. I was inescapably confronted with the reality that all the pleasant things I took for granted as a Westerner, or enjoyed in the exclusive environment of my hotel, were beyond the wildest dreams – let alone the experience – of the average citizen of Mumbai.

Then Bharat, who was a budding tourist guide and evidently enjoyed pointing out landmarks, made a suggestion.

'Sir, the traffic is running smoothly. We should get to the office in plenty of time,' he said.

'That's great – we don't need to be too early, I'm not expected until after nine.'

'In that case, would you like to see something amazing?'

'And what's that?' I asked.

'The world's biggest outdoor laundry,' he said, grinning.

I nodded, bemused. My only previous experience of laundry was our Indesit automatic washing machine back in Macduff, and the ironing board and steam iron for my working shirts.

Bharat pulled the car over and we headed off down a very busy side street, crossed over a small humped-backed railway bridge and past a row of shops and workshops, and stopped at a high brick wall with jagged glass along the top. Bharat pointed at a gap in the wall.

'Over there! Take a look in there, you will be amazed.'

In such dreary, nondescript surroundings, that seemed

highly unlikely, but I did as he said and was met with an utterly amazing sight. This was the Dhobi Ghat public laundry. As far as the eye could see there was an encampment of hundreds of men slaving over open-air troughs of grey water, battering, pounding and scrubbing. Above, them was an array of sheets that looked like an army of massive white flags wafting in the breeze. It was a massive outdoor washing factory – an unbelievable scene of activity that probably hadn't changed in hundreds of years.

After a few minutes of taking snaps, I jumped back into the car and we were soon on our way again. Half an hour later we drove along Tulsi Pipe Road and approached a big wall with iron gates: this was Mafatlal Mills, once one of India's massive textile mills now converted into a commercial and industrial complex. This was home to ABN Amro's Central Enterprise Services, ACES, which was now an Indian division of Royal Bank of Scotland.

Here the security regime was rigorous. Instead of smiles, the expressions were serious and appraising as my papers and RBS security tag were checked and my bag and laptop put through X-ray screening. I understood the need for all of this, and was if anything reassured by the diligence and thoroughness of the staff. But every one of us was oblivious to the imminent terrorist threat that would engulf the city in just over 12 hours' time.

I was first to arrive for our meeting and a receptionist ushered me into a large room. I could see my new face was causing some interest. As the staff arrived, they gathered in groups quietly chatting, but there was an air of expectancy. I began to introduce myself and everyone responded in a very friendly manner.

I was joined by Sean, other senior bank colleagues and some consultants who had been working with us, and we headed down to a modern conference room for my presentation. I was delighted to tell several people they had new jobs within the organisation. There was real pride that they were going into new roles with RBS. I was even getting used to some of the wonderful Indian rituals, but there was one that really made me laugh. Each month all of the employees with birthdays gather in the main office for a joint celebration with birthday cake. Later on in the afternoon, Sean invited me to come along and I agreed. We all trooped upstairs to the office and a large cake dripping with ornate icing, almost like a wedding cake, was cut into segments and shared out. Everyone had a generous slice of cake on their plates and I was about to put a piece into my mouth, when Sean pulled my hand back.

'Rog, you need to watch this first,' he said.

And rather than actually eat the cake, everyone in the room began rubbing it into each other's faces. The uproar of laughter was infectious – and I couldn't stop myself laughing, although I didn't feel comfortable smearing my piece into the faces of people I'd only just become acquainted with. So I ate mine before heading back downstairs. The Indians say the cake ceremony is good luck: it might well have been the mouthfuls that saved my life.

I was delighted that we had now officially set in motion a service in India that was scheduled to open in late December or early January. All the hard work was becoming a reality – and I was satisfied with the progress. I also took more shots of beaming faces with my digital camera for the bank's in-house magazine and it was nearly 7pm when we left the building. Poor Bharat was in a panic because he'd been outside since 6.30 and had just started to worry that I'd left without him and that he might lose his job if something had happened to me. It was nose-to-tail for the next 45 minutes as we crawled

along a few hundred yards to get back on the main road and
headed back to the Oberoi.

Then something very eerie happened. Without any prior
notice, Bharat pulled over to the left of the road and stopped
the car. He came around and opened my door.

'Would you like to have a look at our most famous train
station? It's the Chhatrapati Shivaji Terminus – it's Mumbai's
grand central station.'

I was tired after such a long day and, having been on my
feet most of the time, I declined.

'No thanks. I'd rather get back to the hotel. I've got to
make some calls to my wife and family.'

But Bharat persisted enthusiastically.

'This is an opportunity you will not get very often. It's an
amazing experience at this time of day, and well worth it.'

As it turned out, within the next two hours, this station
was to become the scene of a terrorist bloodbath as gunmen
sprayed bullets across the main concourse, killing at least 50
people. I don't believe Bharat's intentions were sinister in any
way, but fate was kind to me.

I began to think that I'd offended him – but it was now
after 8 and getting dark when he pulled the Merc into a side
street. I clocked the sign: Arthur Bunder Road. Out of the
corner of my eye, I could see someone approaching and he
startled me when he opened the back door.

'Good evening, sir. You're most welcome to visit our
wonderful shop and just look – you can purchase anything
you like later. Please come,' he said.

This really felt like an infringement on my time – and it
was seriously testing my Scottish good humour.

'Look, Bharat, I just want to go back to my hotel,' I said
raising my voice, and pointing at our new friend.

'Ahh, but sir. You will like what you see very much.'

I relented, realising that Bharat was probably poorly paid and reliant on commission for bringing in rich customers. I decided that I didn't have anything pressing, except my calls, so I followed my new-found friend into the Mumbai Bazaar, an air-conditioned emporium. Bharat remained outside. Strangely enough, there were no other customers in the shop. The owner joined us and led me to the back of the store where there were scores of glistering trinkets and displays of costume jewellery and hand-carved stone elephants, but nothing that truly took my eye. Then I spotted a chess set. I was asked if I played and I said, 'A bit', the next thing a dozen boards with elaborate pieces were brought out. There was one stunning set with pieces carved from camel bones and a board of ebony inlaid with what looked like ivory.

'How much would this cost?' I asked with interest.

'About 75,000 rupees.'

That was the equivalent of about a thousand pounds. It was not for me. I felt I had shown enough interest to merit being allowed to leave, but the owner grabbed my arm and led me to shelves of cashmere sweaters, silk brocades, pashminas and printed clothes. It did cross my mind as odd that in this ultra-busy city there was no one else in the shop but I was getting concerned at the amount of time this impromptu browsing was taking up. It had been over an hour since we left Mafatlal Mills and I wanted to go back to the hotel. Now I really wanted out and started to make my way to the door. The owner sensed that an incontrovertible decision had been made and as a last sales pitch gave me a business card, smiled and told me that the store was now online.

In the car on the way back I explained to Bharat that the next day I would need picking up again, and a lift to the airport later, so that I would settle up and give him an extra tip then. He dropped me off and I headed into the hotel. The Oberoi foyer was very busy with parties of new arrivals milling around and heading off into the lobbies and hallways.

CHAPTER NINE

Murderous Mumbai

NORMALLY I WOULD have gone for a wander along the seafront at Nariman Point before going for supper. Tonight, because I'd arrived back much later than expected, I decided to do the opposite and have something to eat first. I freshened up and changed into a clean shirt and a fresh suit. Within about ten minutes I was back downstairs in the Tiffin. There were only one or two diners there. The manager, who I had missed the previous evenings, came over and said hello. She remembered me from my previous visit, even my name, which was sweet.

'Are you back on business or taking a holiday this time, Mr Hunt?' she enquired.

'On business, and it's really lovely being here again. This is a wonderful place,' I said.

'It's very kind of you to say so, Mr Hunt.'

'I mean it – this is one of the best places that I've ever been. I've enjoyed my stay and the service and your food is excellent.'

She smiled and took my order. 'And for your sweet – can we tempt you with one of our delightful Tiffin puddings from the trolley?'

The rich and creamy sweets were pure indulgence – and earlier I had eaten that slab of delicious cake.

'No, I think a main course will do me tonight,' I said. It was a decision that would save my life.

'Would you like a latte or Indian tea perhaps?' she said.

'No thank you, I'm fine,' I replied.

I was keen to have a walk in the cooling night air, then make my phone calls back to Scotland. After my curry and a glass of Indian red wine I wiped my mouth, put the soiled napkin on the table and stood up. And although the restaurant was now filling up, the manager made a point of coming over and wishing me a 'Good evening' as I left.

'Thank you again,' I said. 'I'll see you tomorrow.'

It was just after 9.40pm when I stepped out of the restaurant into the foyer. There was a tremendous buzz coming down the stairs from the Kandahar restaurant on the floor above. As I walked across the hall, I looked over to the bar to the right of the reception where an elegant party of young people in evening wear was gathering.

I headed over to the money exchange so that I'd have enough rupees to tip Bharat for his services, then I walked back across the lobby – and everything appeared to be fine, just what you might expect in this cosmopolitan place: hosts of international guests, young and old, chatting, laughing, sipping cool cocktails or tea in delicate bone china cups, while staff mingled attentively among them. There was the sound of a soothing serenade on piano and violin, the air was fragrant with the aroma of jasmine-scented oil. Then as I stepped into the lift I spotted something incongruous: two young, dark-haired individuals, hurrying across the lobby. Each had a rucksack slung over one shoulder and they looked like backpackers or students – out of the ordinary for this hotel. Next thing, I was startled to see, side on, that one of them was carrying what appeared to be a sub-machine gun – an AK-56 automatic assault rifle, a Chinese version of the infamous Russian AK-47. To my utter and absolute disbelief, the man pointed the gun and opened fire.

Dr-rrrrrrrrr! Dr-rrrrrrr! Dr-rrrrrrrr!

There were three bursts of automatic gunfire.

In the micro-second before the screaming began, I realised I was in the lift and the door was still open. I needed to punch in my floor number before the lift would move. I reached out for the black circle with 14 on it – and quickly hit the button – and then the Door Close button.

Dr-rrrrrrrrr! Dr-rrrrrrrrrr!

There were another two bursts of machine gun fire and utter pandemonium broke out as everyone in the foyer tried to scatter. The screams were ringing out as the lift door closed and carried me upwards, away from the carnage. The sound of another burst of gunfire ricocheted around the foyer. Everywhere people were diving for cover.

My mind was racing at what I had just witnessed. As the lift ascended smoothly to the 14th floor, my initial thought was that this was a hit squad out to get a particular person in an Indian mafia-style feud. I was in shock. I stumbled out, to find a group of my fellow guests peering over the glass balcony down into the atrium below. A man emerged from his room and suggested that it was just some firecrackers being set off as part of an Indian celebration. I put him straight.

'Look, I've just come up from the lobby and there are two guys down there with machine guns. They've already shot and killed people.'

As we all watched in horror over the balcony, the gunmen made their way around the side towards the Tiffin restaurant – and back out into the corridor towards the sister hotel, the Trident. The killing had only just begun.

CHAPTER TEN

The Lobby of Death

IT WAS LIKE one of these scenes from a Hollywood action movie. You might have expected Jean-Claude Van Damme to appear any second. I had to pinch myself to remember that this wasn't a movie; this was deadly serious.

The gunmen I had seen were continuing to spray their fire indiscriminately, and now they were also lobbing hand grenades into the midst of the panic-stricken people. I had seen two gunmen before, but now I knew there were at least three of them, possibly a lot more. Hunched down, I watched with horror as one of them turned into the Tiffin restaurant. I strained to see what was happening but my view was partially obscured by the balcony. I could hear the shots that were being drilled out of the gun and my whole spine froze with a sensation of fear such as I had never experienced.

Less than a few minutes ago, I myself had been dining in the Tiffin.

Guests and staff were being mown down in front of my eyes. What had been a luxurious hotel was now an orgy of bloody carnage. The whole building echoed to the sound of gunfire. And then I saw Alan Scherr and his daughter Naomi being hit by bullets. *Oh, my God!* The young girl I'd watched only yesterday evening in the swimming pool, so full of fun and without a care in the world, was now caught up in this awful event. Her father was lying still. I could see a gaping wound in his head. His daughter's limp body lay beside him. I could see a dark red pool of blood spreading out across the floor. It was ghastly.

I found out that about two dozen people from their group, the Synchronicity Foundation from Virginia, had gathered in the Kandahar for their evening meal.

A British eyewitness, Alex Chamberlen, who works for an Indian cricketing website, later said one of the gunmen, aged about 22 or 23 and speaking Urdu or Hindi, had ordered 30 to 40 people from the stairway into the restaurant: 'A guy burst into the Kandahar with a machine gun. He was in western dress and wearing jeans, and he asked for British and American tourists. He told everybody to stop and put their hands up. My friend said to me, "Don't be hero, don't say you're British".'

Another eyewitness, Rajesh Patel, who worked for the HSBC bank, later told reporters: 'Three men came into the hotel. They were young, around 20 years old. And they started rounding up foreigners that were eating there. They told everyone to drop their phones and to "come with us", then at that point the blast happened.'

A businessman, Colin Tungate, must have been in one of the other lifts as this was unfolding. He told reporters that he had just reached the lobby when the shooting began. A Japanese man was shot and wounded and Mr Tungate had the frantic task of moving the wounded man's foot from the door as he tried to close the lift and escape.

It would emerge that the attackers had come in by sea from the Pakistani city of Karachi. A few days earlier they had hijacked an Indian fishing trawler and murdered all of the crew, except the captain, who had been forced to take them to Mumbai. He was beheaded as they neared their destination. To avoid Indian security and customs, the terrorists boarded two inflatables and landed near the Gateway of India, which is beside Bombay harbour and near the Taj Mahal Palace & Tower Hotel, at 9.20pm, under cover of darkness. They then split off into three groups to begin their attacks.

Of course we knew nothing of this. More people were streaming out of their rooms. But when they realised the awful situation, most retreated. There was no discussion. With the chaos unfolding below, it seemed the only sensible thing to do. I headed to my door, pushed in my key and entered the room. Downstairs, the screaming, shouting, shooting and killing was still going on.

I stood inside the door, my chest heaving with anxiety. *Keep cool. Keep cool. Keep your head clear*, I said to myself. At least it was a heavy wooden door that would require a lot of strength to force open. What now? What do you do in a situation like this? A situation that no one ever prepares you for unless you join the armed forces? A situation far removed from the normal experience of a banker from Scotland?

After a few moments, I went to open the safe in the dressing room. With everything I'd just witnessed still computing in my brain, I struggled to remember the combination. But eventually I recalled the right sequence and removed my British passport, my car keys and flight tickets from Mumbai to Heathrow, and then on to Aberdeen. Nothing else was important to me. I didn't even pick up my wallet. Survival instinct was beginning to kick in. I stuffed all this into my pockets.

I could still hear gunfire and there were several more grenade explosions. The screaming had died down. Now from outside the bedroom window was the wailing of sirens from somewhere far off, getting nearer and nearer.

I heard a scraping sound in the room to the left. It was as if a heavy piece of furniture was being dragged across the floor and propped up against the door. I guessed the man there was barricading his door. He was not the only one to take this course of action. Later I heard that a British lawyer, Mark Abell, one of two partners from law firm Field Fisher Waterhouse who were on the 23rd floor of the hotel, told the BBC from his room: 'There's no escape. I have barricaded my door with furniture. It's not the most pleasant of experiences but I suppose it is a question of the British stiff upper lip. It would be foolhardy to leave, so I am sitting reading and trying to ignore what is going on.'

He had been in the Kandahar with his colleague Chris Jackson and left about 30 minutes before the attack. After dinner he had been chatting in the lobby with some Japanese businessmen waiting for the lift. 'The lifts are usually slow but that day they were fast. I got the lift to my room and after 10 minutes I heard a big blast. I think one of the Japanese men was killed in the blast.'

Like me, Mark Abell was stranded for over 40 hours in his room. In retrospect, I admire his calm and that English stiff upper lip; while he was sitting reading quietly in his room, I was absolutely petrified.

It appears the Japanese victim he mentions was Hisashi Tsuda, a 38-year-old Japanese businessman, working for Mitsui Marubeni Liquefied Gas Company, who was shot in the chest, stomach and leg, near the front desk. He died later from his wounds. His colleague, Tatsuya Kessoku sustained minor injuries.

There were many international victims in the Oberoi's bloody lobby that evening, including Brett Taylor, a 49-year-old timber merchant, and Doug Markell, 71, both from Sydney, Australia, and Antonio de Lorenzo, a businessman from Livorno in Italy. The tributes for Brett were moving. *The Age* newspaper in Melbourne described him as a devoted family man, a 'Great Australian' and 'a man of his word'. One of his mates said: 'He was a kind, generous, positive bloke, just incredibly hard-working.'

To me, he sounds like a down-to-earth individual caught up in a horrific global incident; a good man in a truly hellish place.

CHAPTER ELEVEN

Survival Tactics

I WAS ALONE, far from home, trapped in this darkened Mumbai hotel room. What do you do when you are stuck in a siege? What are the tactics for survival? Is it the luck of the draw, or are their some tiny, incremental things you can do to increase your chances of staying alive?

I had no idea of the real situation. Or how long I might be holed up. At first I thought of switching on the television news channels to at least gain an idea of what might be happening, but common sense overrode that idea. Switching on a TV would almost certainly be a surefire indication that a Westerner was occupying the room.

I devised and adapted my own strategy for survival as I went along. It was pretty raw and instinctive. I decided to remain in my room and not to barricade the door, although I shivered when I heard nearby scuffling noises that told me the gunmen were very close. I realised that the terrorists were still in control, scouring the hotel, floor by floor, room by room, for Western visitors.

My initial belief that the attack in the lobby was some sort of local gang feud that would all be over quickly now gave way, and I began to have an inkling that it was a terrorist assault with westerners and those living a more western lifestyle the prime targets. As yet I had no idea this was part of a concerted attack across the city which was already making international headlines.

It was well into the evening and the curtains and the screens at the window were closed. I switched off the lights as well, then I changed into my jeans; this would be more practical for moving around inside the room and attempting my escape. I also figured that if a gunman was searching a room at a time, he might take a cursory look in the door. If it looked as if the room was dark and empty, the bed made and no personal belongings in the cupboard or on display on the bedside table, then he would quickly move on.

My thought was to make a hiding place and tuck myself out of sight. So I made the bed, turning it down as if it was awaiting a guest. I cleared all my toilet gear back into its bag and put it out of sight in the bathroom. I scrutinised every inch of the room looking for somewhere that I could conceal myself. I pulled out the drawers from the units to see if there was enough space to hide down the back. There wasn't. I tried climbing into the top of the wardrobe but the solid partition in the top section meant that the space was too tight.

I ruled out hiding in the wardrobe or under the bed, which were too obvious. So I heaved the heavy couch into a corner and placed it so that it made a barricade. I checked the room once more for any telltale signs, then I climbed in behind the settee and hunkered down out of sight in the triangle of space. It was very tight but I was well concealed.

I was tempted to remove all the drinks, especially the water and soft drinks, from the minibar, but I realised that in modern hotels the payment system is linked to the central computer. The drinks in the fridge are stored on a sensitive pad and once they are removed it sparks a payment note. If the killers were in control of the reception area, I surmised they could watch and wait for any movement. Then hunt down the room.

Back in Edinburgh there were a group of my friends and colleagues who knew about my work in Mumbai. Now I needed to alert them to my situation. In Gogarburn, there was Lesley Laird who worked in Policy & Advice Services as a client relationship manager, her colleagues Lorraine Kneebone, a customer operations manager, and Karlynn Sokoluk. I'd emailed Lesley earlier to tell her the day had gone well at ACES. I told her I'd been enjoying a brilliant Indian Cabernet Sauvignon.

It had only been about seven minutes since I had left the restaurant but it seemed like an age. I needed to alert them using my Blackberry. I bet when the Canadian Mike Lazaridis invented this wonderful device in 1999, he had no idea how important and lifesaving it would become. While it includes a mobile phone, its real selling point was that it allowed you to email on the move – any time, anywhere that had a proper signal. Thankfully, India is a well-connected nation for the technophiles. This humble black and silver machine with its lighted screen and mini Qwerty keyboard was my lifeline to the outside world. I held it close to my chest so that the light on the screen would not radiate out.

Throughout my ordeal, it allowed me to send and receive text messages and emails when it was too risky to make a sound or use my other mobile phone. I quickly typed in a very simple SOS.

From: Roger Hunt
Sent: Wednesday 26 November 2008 16:47
To: Lesley Laird, Lorraine Kneebone; Andrew Penker
Subject: Re: Hello
Lesley. Please do not treat this as a joke. The hotel that

I am in has been attacked. People have been shot dead and large explosions are going on. I have fears for my life. Can you advise someone please.

I pressed the SEND button – and off it went. That was all I said. It was my first message in a stream that would keep up my spirits. At the same time, I also pinged a message to Karlynn, because I thought Lesley might not be at her desk to pick up my SOS. I wanted her to call Irene and let her know that I had made contact. The subject: 'Customer Insights Survey' referred to an earlier email – and it was so much simpler and quicker just to hit the REPLY button than begin a new email from scratch.

From: Roger Hunt
Sent: Wednesday 26 November 2008 16:50
To: Karlynn Sokoluk
Subject: Re: Customer Insights Survey
Hi. If you pick this up can you speak to Lesley and call my wife as a matter of urgency! Pls

Lesley is a reliable and efficient person, very on the ball. She knows I like a joke, but I wanted her to understand the gravity of my predicament. I didn't have to wait long for her reply.

From: Lesley Laird
Sent: Wednesday 26 November 2008 16:53
To: Roger Hunt
Subject: RE: Hello
Hi Rog... On the case. Now.

There was now a sense of alarm and urgency in the bank HQ in Edinburgh.

From: Karlynn Sokoluk
Sent: Wednesday 26 November 16:58

To: Roger Hunt
Subject: RE: Customer Insights Survey
Whats up... what message do you want to give?
K

I sent a response to Karlynn asking her to refer to Lesley saying simply: 'Hotel Under Attack'.

From: Lesley Laird
Sent: Wednesday 26 November 16:54
To: Roger Hunt
Subject: What hotel are you in?

I didn't have time to reply. There was an almighty explosion. It was earth-shatteringly louder than the noise of the grenades. It was like being in the epicentre of an earthquake. The room was shuddering, there was a swoosh of air and then I heard an avalanche of glass shattering outside. It felt as if the whole building was about to collapse. Instantly, the hotel fire alarms went off, but no water sprayed from the sprinkler system.

I lay on the floor, increasingly stunned about what was happening. I thought this was the end for me. It was only later that I learned that the terrorists had laid 9kg of RDX high explosives outside the hotel. Their improvised explosive device was designed to make a lot of mess – it was packed with ball bearings to create shrapnel.

When I raised my head from behind the couch, I could see that the room was starting to fill with smoke. At first it came in from under the door, then black, acrid fumes began to come through the walls. I started to cough as the grit stuck in my throat.

The situation was getting much more desperate than I had first thought. I could hear screams in the street. I remained pinned to the floor. Clutching my Blackberry and mobile phone, with a towel wrapped round my hands, I could feel the room getting warmer. The floor was heating up, which meant there must be a blaze down below. I rushed into the bathroom, grabbed a large bath towel and placed it at the front door to cut down the smoke. There was no water when I turned on the taps: I found out later that the gunmen had managed to switch off the supply. I was starting to gasp for breath.

From: Roger Hunt
Sent: Wednesday 26 November 16:55
To: Lesley Laird
Subject: Re: What hotel are you in?
Oberoi in Mumbai. Explosions noow.

From: Lesley Laird
Sent: Wednesday 26 November 16:56
To: Roger Hunt
Subject: RE: What hotel are you in?
On to alert line now.

From: Lesley Laird
Sent: Wednesday 26 November 17:04
To: Roger Hunt
Subject: Are you ok...
Have contacted alertline. They will contact their people in India now. More to follow.

From: Lesley Laird
Sent: Wednesday 26 November 17:10
To: Roger Hunt
Subject: R U OK???

From: Andrew Sharman
Sent: Wednesday 26 November 17:14
To: Roger Hunt

Subject: RE: Hello
Hi Rog
Went immed to Lesley and she is trying to help.

The explosions were frightening. It felt as if the raw nerves in my head were being scraped by a sharpened screwdriver. I wanted out... now.

CHAPTER TWELVE

HQ Kicks into Action

IT WAS A TYPICAL mid-week afternoon in Edinburgh. Wednesday was Lynne Highway's day for picking up her two boys, Kieran, who was eleven, and Ross, who was seven, from their after-school club in Edinburgh. She had just gone into the cloakroom area in House A at Gogarburn and was pulling on her coat, ready for her getaway at 4.45pm. She was dashing out to beat the traffic, which is often congested because of RBS staff leaving and general airport traffic during the evening rush hour. She was picking up her bag when her PA, Ann Hanson, approached. Her face looked very serious, and she was holding the print-out of an email.

'I've just received this from Lesley. There's something going on in Roger's hotel. It seems as if there is a fire at his hotel,' she said.

Lynne, who has a polite air of purpose that really motivates people, read the email and immediately started to delegate some instructions, but then Lesley appeared in person from downstairs with an updated email, which looked much more serious. Call it intuition, but both Lesley and Lynne knew this wasn't some trivial hotel fire – this was something much more significant. What, though, they did not know. Lynne never reached the front door that evening. It would be another two days before she made it back home. She re-hung her coat on the hangers and went downstairs to find out what exactly was going on. In the P&A area there was a great murmur of noise and chat, and a range of garbled and confusing messages. She sensed there was too much uncoordinated activity going on. 'Hold on, hold on, hold on,' said Lynne. 'Let's get some kind of order into this.'

She calmed my colleagues, directing each member to make the right calls and contacts to set in motion the correct procedures for a serious incident. Lynne was purely following the protocols set up by the bank in case of an emergency, and insuring that some kind of structured chain of command would do its very best to keep its staff safe and alive.

My bank colleagues still thought it was a local fire at the hotel. There were no television screens in the open-plan area, but one or two colleagues were browsing Google to see if there was any indication of an incident in Mumbai. As 5pm approached, there was nothing concrete to report.

Lynne directed the team as they made a number of calls to RBS's internal security service and fraud department, which handles major incidents. Ann phoned Lynne's mother, Janis, who went to collect the boys from the after-school club. Lynne's notebook was out and she compiled a 'Must-Do' list with 'Phone Roger's wife Irene' at the top.

Back on the first floor, Lynne went into the next office to speak to Elaine Arden, a colleague who had recently been out in India and stayed at the Oberoi. She explained the hotel lay-out and this helped Lynne to visualise the place. Downstairs, the email trail was beginning to hot up.

From: Karlynn Sokoluk
Sent: Wednesday 26 November 17:15
To: Roger Hunt
Subject: RE: Customer Insights Survey

Rog
Hopefully you can pick this message up. Please let us know you are okay, take care of yourself. Karlynn

From: Roger Hunt
Sent: Wednesday 26 November 17:17
To: Lesley Laird
Subject: Re: R U OK???
No. Building on fire and trapped in my room. Still shooting.

From: Lesley Laird
Sent: Wednesday 26 November 17:17
To: Roger Hunt
Subject: Update for you
We are looking to get more info and to contact our people in India. Lynne and John on the case.
Is there anything else we can do?
In case you can use this – Alertline is your emergency helpline. Your safety is our top priority...

Shooting? What kind of shooting? There was a growing sense of disbelief. Not because they thought I was joking: it just took a while to sink in. But it was becoming increasingly apparent that this might be a terrorist action.

Alertline is RBS's group-wide response which deals with corporate or personal matters. But what was most reassuring to me was that the bank's systems were starting to mobilise. It all required control and concentration, rather than sporadic actions. In normal circumstances, a bank is in its element in a situation of high tension dealing with complex matters – but this was an abnormal situation.

Lynne's job was to dampen down any creeping sense of panic that might be setting in across the team. She wanted people to stay calm, although inside she was flapping with her own emotions, knowing it had been her decision to dispatch me to Mumbai.

She needed to set up an incident room away from the general background noise of a bank that needed to continue with its day-to-day business. She was able to commandeer Room NI/I in House A. It became the nerve centre of the operation to get me back safely. On one wall there was a giant screen and on the table a projector and phone hub for audio conferences. There was a solid wooden table with eight chairs, in orange fabric and with metal sides and legs. The team ripped out several sheets of A2 paper from a flipchart and then stuck them with tape over the window. No one in the corridor could see into the room.

Gavin Reid was RBS's main man in India, and he was immediately informed of the situation. Gavin was with Mhairi Thomson, a friend and colleague of mine who had only arrived in Mumbai that afternoon. She had been tired after her trip but Gavin, who is an assiduous host, insisted on taking her out for a drink to introduce her to a group of bank people and show her the sights. This proved to be a stroke of good fortune for Mhairi. They had booked a table at Mahesh's restaurant, well-known for its wonderful seafood, which is a speciality of South Mumbai.

RBS has a crisis management approach which was well-tested – five weeks earlier it had been in full flight when it dealt with the massive impact of the global banking crisis which had caused the bank's near collapse, and the resulting emergency bail-out by the UK government. That was one kind of disaster recovery: but this was an entirely different matter. In this case, an incident control group was set up and a number of different bank departments, including security and fraud, were involved. It was all quickly in place with Lynne leading the show. Downstairs, my colleagues were hungry for any snippet of information. By now the newsflashes were beginning to appear on BBC News 24 with the red tickertape across the bottom of the screen reading: BREAKING NEWS: TERRORIST ATTACK IN MUMBAI. As the team awaited an update from Lynne, they simply refused to go home. I always knew they were a stubborn lot.

They became part of the bank's vigil for me. And there was another factor for the Human Resources team to consider. I wasn't necessarily the only bank employee caught up in this situation. RBS had dozens of British people working in Mumbai on various integration projects, on top of which there was a whole host of new Indian colleagues working for ABN Amro, who were now part of the enlarged RBS. The group became concerned about their welfare and safety throughout the rest of the city. While much of this was looked after by local management in Mumbai, using the same structures and linking into the UK, the 'HR Silver Team' kicked in to scour staff records to work out where everybody was.

The Mumbai incident was quickly taken to the very top of the organisation. Lynne had alerted Neil Roden, the Group head of HR. He in turn informed the board and Sir Fred Goodwin, who had his own personal battles to fight at the time. He asked to be kept up to speed. All that night Neil Roden was updated as news filtered through, and a group executive also chaired the incident control committee. The RBS team was to play a vital role in helping me keep my nerve and hold onto my wits – not to mention my sanity – in the deadly ordeal that had only started to unfold.

CHAPTER THIRTEEN

Phoning Home

THE SITUATION IN ROOM 1478 was getting worse. The heat was now unbearable and a wall of thick acrid smoke had filled the room. Perhaps I could force open the window and jump from the 14th floor? I climbed in behind the full-length curtain and screen which gave me a few moments of clearer air. I stood on the window sill but there was no opening; the reinforced plate-glass windows were sealed shut. And there was no balcony.

It was a sheer drop from the 14th floor.

I squinted along the street. I could see that a large crowd had gathered. It was being held back by police in brown uniforms and security service people, some wearing blue helmets with plastic anti-riot protectors, and armed with old British army-style, bolt-action rifles. They were looking up at the hotel. I was heartened when I saw a large red and grey fire engine emerge on my side of the building with its ladders extending. That gave me a sense of hope. At last, the Indian authorities were in action; hopefully they might be able to regain control.

If I could attract the attention of anyone down on the street, it might mean they could direct the ladders to me and I'd be rescued quickly. By now it was dark outside, so I switched on my two mobile phones with the background lights shining and began to wave my arms in the air, slowly criss-crossing with the phones in my hands. It took about five minutes before anyone saw me. Meanwhile the smoke was getting thicker. I could see a television crew below with their camera and mobile searchlight trained on the hotel. Over at the ABN Amro building the office lights were still burning brightly and I could make out figures at the windows.

Then I was spotted by some Indian passers-by running along beneath my window. One of them stopped and looked up, shouting and calling at me.

I couldn't really hear what was being said. But I could read his body language. And my heart sank as he waved and shouted for me to get back into my room. 'Not safe! Not safe!' he appeared to be yelling. And as I looked over the fire engine began moving off, turning away from the building – and my window.

To my complete horror, the police were waving the fire engine away from the Oberoi. It disappeared out of view. *What the hell was happening? Why was it being turned away?* There was no way I was going to be rescued in time by the fire brigade now. There was a terrible sinking feeling in the pit of my stomach; I conceded that the situation was now so grave that I was likely to die in this burning room. Instinctively, I picked up the Blackberry.

From: Roger Hunt
Sent: Wednesday 26 November 17:18
To: Lesley Laird
Subject: Re: Update for you
Please phone my wife. Love her and kids.

Lesley will never know how welcome and reassuring her simple reply was to me.

From: Lesley Laird
Sent: Wednesday 26 November 17:19
To: Roger Hunt
Subject: RE: Update for you
OK – will do.

I had this overwhelming urge to try and phone Irene. If these were my last moments on earth I wanted to let her know what I felt about her: that I loved her now even more than on our wedding day. There was so much I wanted to say. But I realised I could not put her through such distress. I felt as long as I could still breathe, I did not want to make that heartbreaking call.

From: Lesley Laird
Sent: Wednesday 26 November 17:20
To: Roger Hunt
Subject: RE: R U OK???
Can you use your phone. Gavin Reid is just across the street.
L

From: Lesley Laird
Sent: Wednesday 26 November 2008 17:22
To: Roger Hunt
Subject: This is Gavin's telephone number 0777000000000.
Might need 0044 then 77.

From: Lesley Laird
Sent: Wednesday 26 November 17:33
To: Roger Hunt
Subject: Any more news...

From: Roger Hunt
Sent: Wednesday 26 November 17:43

To: Lesley Laird
Subject: Re: Any more news...
Trapped in smoke and vomiting and can't break window
get Gav to call my mobile.

From: Lesley Laird
Sent: Wednesday 26 November 17:45
To: Roger Hunt
Subject: RE: Any more news...
Rog – we are here and doing our best to get things mov-
ing for you. Hang on... Can you use something to smash
the window – wet towels on the floor and stay low. Put a
wet towel on your head. Stay low as you can... L

Then another of my colleagues passed on some advice. Wes Beattie was an ex-inspector in the Hong Kong police, so he knew a thing or two about survival.

From: Wesley Beattie
Sent: Wednesday 26 November 17:48
To: Roger Hunt
Subject: Roger – Lynnes speaking to your wife
Stay down, and towels at the crack in the door, fill the
bath... Use something to break the window if you can...

Back in Macduff, my family were sitting down in our kitchen to have their tea. Irene had finished her work at the school at 2.30pm, bought some messages and headed home to make the tea. It was Stephanie's Highland dancing night and Irene normally took it in turns with a friend to drop her off in the car.

At about 5.30pm, Irene was dishing up a bowl of lentil soup followed by mince and tatties for her dad, Lisa, Christopher and Stephanie. Irene wasn't 100 per cent – she had a strange feeling in her stomach. She actually felt sick but couldn't think what it might be: it was a horrible feeling that was putting her off her food.

Our bulky old television with the video player was flickering in the corner with the sound turned down. The dining table chat turned to me and they began to speak about when I'd be making my daily phone call. I had phoned at 6pm on the Monday and told them all about the Indian wedding. The joke is that I've usually got some story to tell. That escapade had them all laughing. Typical Roger, said Irene. I'd explained to her that I wouldn't phone on Tuesday because I was going out for dinner with Gavin, but it would be the same time on Wednesday.

So the family were waiting for my routine call. When I've been away I'm normally like clockwork, phoning every night at around the same time. Irene forced herself to finish her soup, and then scrapped at the potatoes on the plate.

At about 5.40pm the phone rang and Irene stood up and leaned over to answer it.

'Ah, this'll be him. He's early,' she said.

But it wasn't me; it was Lynne Highway.

'Hi, this is Lynne Highway. I'm one of Roger's colleagues at RBS in Edinburgh,' she said.

'Ohh! Hello,' said Irene. She had heard me speaking about Lynne, but had never actually met her or spoken to her before.

'Roger has been in contact with us from Mumbai,' Lynne said.

Irene took a moment to compute what was happening and thought perhaps I'd taken ill. She recalled that I'd had a sore throat when I left on the Sunday.

But Lynne continued, 'We know that Roger is in his room and there's been a fire in the lobby of the hotel. There's been some sort of gunfire – but we're not sure what that is.'

'Thank you – thanks. OK, right, thank you for phoning,' said Irene nervously, still not really understanding what was being said.

Lynne sensed the shock. 'Irene, are you in the house on your own?' she asked.

That's the kind of question you ask someone when they've been given bad news, isn't it? It was then that it dawned on Irene that this was something serious. It struck home. And she started to cry. Seeing Irene in tears, the others started to pay attention. Irene's dad and Stephanie had been chatting at the table, Christopher was mooching in the cupboards for a chocolate biscuit, Lisa had opened her laptop to get on with her work placement project.

Lisa could tell from Irene's voice that something wasn't right.

'What's happening, Mum, what's going on?'

'Wheeeest!' said Irene, raising her hand and telling everyone to keep quiet because she was still listening to Lynne's voice.

Thinking this was funny, Stephanie and Christopher both laughed before hearing Irene's next question.

'Is Roger safe?'

'At the moment, he's in his hotel room. We think he's safe but we don't know a great deal,' replied Lynne.

Irene's stony face relayed the gravity of this phone call to everyone. Lynne told Irene that the story would be breaking on Sky News and she wanted to let her know first.

Irene shouted to Stephanie.

'Can you turn over to the Sky News channel? There's something happening in India, where your dad is working.'

We're not short of television sets in our house and we'd recently become Sky TV subscribers because of the live football and the movies that Irene and I like to watch. There was a small portable TV in the corner of the kitchen.

'OK, Mum, I'll do it right away,' replied Stephanie.

Lynne explained that an incident room had been set up in Edinburgh and there were people working for the bank on the ground out in Mumbai.

'We're doing everything in our power to get Roger out safely and back to Scotland as soon as possible,' said Lynne.

She then asked to speak to Irene's dad, to make sure everything was being taken in. After all, this wasn't the usual teatime call. He spoke to Lynne, listening and nodding, before handing back to Irene.

'OK, Irene. I'll be your regular contact. I'll keep you up-to-date with what's happening every half an hour and I'll let you know how things are progressing.'

This first call took less than five minutes. Irene put the phone down, but didn't fully appreciate how serious the situation was. How could she? Nobody did. Not even me, and I had just witnessed people being slaughtered. She felt nauseous, but imagined that within the hour there would be another call to say 'He's out,' and Roger would have another great story to tell about another scrape.

In Edinburgh, Lynne came off the phone and sent me a message:

> Rog all thinking about you. Have spoken to Irene and her Dad and making sure she is OK as best we can. Doing everything we can to get you out of there. Reply if you can. Love Lynne.

The television was now switched onto Sky News – and there were night-time images of a hotel on fire. This wasn't the Oberoi though. This was the Taj Mahal Palace & Tower Hotel, just around the corner. There was thick black smoke pouring out of this beautiful domed building, and underneath a strip saying: Breaking News: Terror attack at Mumbai hotel: Reports of gunfire.

After half an hour, there was another call from Lynne. There wasn't really anything new to add, but Lynne was reassuring. Meanwhile Lisa phoned Irene's friend Caren, whose turn it was to take Stephanie and her own daughter Erin, to their dancing class. Lisa said Stephanie had decided she wasn't going to go tonight and explained what was happening. Caren inquired if everything was OK, then Irene took the phone. She was now quite shaken, and said that they were simply waiting for news. Irene phoned her sister, Carole, while Albert, her dad, went back to his house to switch off his lights. He had sensed that this might take some time. Then Irene's other sister, Karine, phoned; she too was on her way. An hour went by with the news still showing images of the fires, but there was no clear picture of what was happening. With every minute that passed, Irene began to worry more and more. She became so wound up she rushed into the bathroom, feeling as if she might throw up, retched, but wasn't actually sick. She didn't want to worry anyone about her, so she wiped her mouth with a flannel, rejoined the rest and said nothing. Within a short time, her close-knit family had gathered *en masse* in Corskie Drive: her dad, her two sisters, then her cousin, Brenda and her husband, Robbie, all came round to give support.

Throughout my ordeal, Lynne Highway was a solid rock. I can never thank her enough. She passed on titbits of news, while any specific information on my position was passed back to MI5 agents who were coordinating plans with the Indian Army's elite Black Cats Commandos to get me out. She worked through the night on Wednesday and all through Thursday. She recalled later that she thought the world had gone nuts. Lynne phoned her mum and said goodnight to her two boys, and explained she wasn't going to get back. She spoke to her husband, Andy, who was on a late shift, and he headed off home.

The hours went by and still I was holed up and my messages intermittent. Lynne's PA nipped downstairs to the store in the RBS complex to get some toiletries so she didn't have to go home. Meanwhile, Lynne sipped cups of peppermint tea, while her colleagues nibbled at sandwiches and drank Coke. Lynne felt a strong sense of duty towards keeping Irene informed. She felt Irene had enough to cope with without being passed on to other banking colleagues she might not know. She told me later that she believed I would have done exactly the same in a similar situation. She was right about that.

Lynne also wanted to reassure my colleagues downstairs that everything was being done to ensure my safety.

Back in Room 1478, I was fighting for my life.

From: Karlynn Sokoluk
Sent: Wednesday 26 November 17:49
To: Roger Hunt
Subject: Smash the windows, get as low on the ground, cover your face with wet towel

Having watched the fire engine disappear, I risked making a single phone call to Gavin. He was in the middle of his meal at Mahesh's and still under the impression that it was a fire, rather than a terrorist attack.

'What's happening, Gavin? It's desperate in here,' I whispered, crouched in my hiding place behind the couch.

'Rog, get out. Get out now. Get out and head to the fire escape. I understand the place is on fire.'

'Tell the fire services on the ground my room location. Please, please...'

My head was spinning and I was coughing and gasping for fresh oxygen. I could still hear Gavin shouting, almost screaming instructions at me. But I felt an overwhelming sickness. I was retching and choking. I had to get air, some air. I just hung up the phone. And I was physically sick. The choking filled me with immense fear. I could not breathe and I knew I was going to die.

What goes on in a human mind when there are so few options? I was sure I would not survive, it was simply a matter of how I would be killed. My thoughts turned to a recent programme I had watched with grim fascination about 'The Falling Man of 9/11', the story of the tragic, iconic figure of a man falling from the burning Twin Towers after the terrorist attack in New York on 11 September 2001. Many people jumped to their death that day, but this single image captured the intense horror of the situation.

I remember Irene and myself in the comfort of our own sitting room debating in theory what we would do in this situation. We both agreed that jumping to certain death would have taken some terrible resolve. But now, in my hotel room, I had no idea that the death of that Falling Man was connected to me; that the global battle between Muslim extremists and the West was still going on – and that this evening the focus was Mumbai. Back on our settee in Macduff I had told Irene I could never jump, not as long as there was a spasm of life left in me. And now I knew that even if I could muster the strength to smash the window, jumping was instant death. Yet I knew that if I left the room I faced almost certain death at the hands of the gunmen. I calculated that as long as they were on the loose my best chance was to stay put and hope that the fire would not engulf me. But the smoke was already so thick I could see no further than the writing bureau just a couple of feet away. Beyond was a black void filled with smoke.

I had inhaled more smoke and I vomited again. My stomach was sore with the involuntary retching. I needed to get some vital fresh air into the room, although I knew that oxygen simply fuels fire. I felt my way to the chair and lifted it up. It was solid and heavy and I struggled to lift it above my head. Several times I smashed the chair against the window, bashing with all the force I could muster, yet the thick plate-glass would not break.

My only other option was to take my chances with the gunmen on the loose. I tried to gather my thoughts. I began to calculate how many rooms were in the hotels. I thought perhaps about 300. If I stayed in the room I had a 300 to 1 chance of surviving death from a bullet. On the other hand, I felt that opening the door and venturing out into the lobby would be imminent death.

The smoke and fumes were overpowering me. I got as low as I could on the floor and crawled along, fumbling for anything that could help me. I managed to reach a table where there was a fruit bowl, a small knife and a white cotton hand towel, which I had used to cut some fresh plums early that day. I grabbed the hand towel.

What I did next would have disgusted me in normal circumstances. I undid my trousers and urinated on the towel. It wasn't pleasant but was my only chance. It was instinctive. With no water from the taps, I had to do this, making the hand towel as wet as I could. I placed the sodden towel with the bitter stench of my own pee over my mouth and face, and covered my head with it. Then I crawled back in behind my couch, which was now a makeshift bomb shelter.

The moisture gave me a moment's relief. I had one of those acute moments when something clicks in your brain; I realised the smoke wasn't coming in under the door, it was the air conditioning that was streaming the dark fumes into my room. I had to get to the switch.

I eased out from behind my shelter, but I could not see a

thing. It was extremely hot and dark, and you could have cut the fumes with a knife. But I had a sense of the layout and I dragged myself purposefully along the carpet.

It took a few minutes feeling my way until I reached the opposite wall. I felt with my hands up towards the switches. Rising onto my feet I reached a box on the wall, which I knew must be the air-con control. My fingers brushed over the panel and I worked out which switch to press. I pushed the button, and the fan clicked and shut down immediately.

Still holding the stinking towel to my face, I dropped back down to the floor and crawled back to the couch. This was all a concerted action that literally gave me breathing space. Already the smoke was beginning to abate.

From: Lesley Laird
Sent: Wednesday 26 November 17:55
To: Roger Hunt
Subject: Still here for you...

From: Lesley Laird
Sent: Wednesday 26 November 18:01
To: Roger Hunt
Subject: R U STILL OK?????

From: Lesley Laird
Sent: Wednesday 26 November 18:05
To: Roger Hunt
Subject: Help on its way...
Full incident management underway. Team being sent by Control Risk. What room/ floor are you in?

The message from the incident team gave me fresh hope. I was working for a major global organisation, surely they would be able to pull out the stops? The weight of such a company in my corner gave me a certain strength.

As I lay on the floor behind the couch, the email and text messages flooded in from friends and colleagues across the world. I had an overwhelming urge to contact Irene: I wanted her to know I loved her. But there was one particular email that brought huge big tears to my eyes.

A message came in from Mary Wilson and her husband Willie, who lived two doors down from us in Corskie Drive. Mary also worked for RBS and was the manager in the local Banff branch. She was a long-standing family friend. Her message said Lisa had gone in to see them. I pictured her sitting with them in their immaculately tidy living room. I imagined this slim, fair-haired young woman, my daughter, trying frantically to get some signal that I was alive. They simply wanted to know if I was OK and could I reply. I stared at that email for some time. The picture in my mind was so real, I held out a hand to try and touch Lisa. I was lying on my side and I could taste the salt in my mouth from the tears. I was tempted to phone or drop a reply. But I didn't want to say I was fine, raising false hope, when things were grim indeed. I didn't want to give them hope when at any time things could go badly wrong.

This was a horrible decision to make and perhaps my family might think it rather heartless, especially when the family vigil back in Banffshire was desperate for any snippet from me. But I was firm in my view. I believed contacting family and friends to raise false hopes was not the right thing to do.

Lynne kept her word to Irene, phoning every half hour on the button. But there was still very little concrete news.

'He's still in his room. We're doing all we can,' was really as much as Lynne could add.

While it was the wee small hours of Thursday in Mumbai, in Scotland it was 8 on Wednesday evening. Irene and Lynne decided to make the calls hourly, unless something major was happening. Irene still thought that I would be home soon; but she phoned her work colleague and close friend Heather to say she wasn't going to be at work the next day, and to let her boss know.

In her mind, she wanted to be in the house when I came back. Heather and her husband, James, are another couple who are great friends of ours in close-knit Macduff. We go out regularly together to the local bowling club. The local phone calls in Macduff didn't stop and more wellwishers had turned up to give Irene support, including her brother, John, and his partner, Jacqueline. Neighbours and friends were coming and going with the kettle working overtime as tea, coffee and biscuits were made and dispensed by Carole and Karine.

Irene had also been in touch with my mum and dad, and they had contacted my own sister Lynne, who was now living in Abu Dhabi with her husband, John. My sister texted and phoned Lisa for regular updates and John offered to fly to Mumbai and help get me out. He even phoned a friend who knew someone working in the Oberoi. They got through to this unnamed person who told them that I was on the 14th floor and I was 'safe'. This was relayed back to John. How he got that precise information, I never found out. But it was decided that John would be better staying put, rather than have another family member caught in the carnage.

The horror unfolded in our Macduff living room through the lenses of the Sky News, BBC and ITN cameramen on the ground in Mumbai. Then the image of one of the gunmen appeared – he was wearing a Versace T-shirt and his eyes were glazed with hatred. The Sky News strip read: Breaking News: Indian TV Reports Confrontation Between Gunmen and Police Outside Hospital. Then there were startling eyewitness accounts from people trapped in the Taj Mahal, including Sajjad Karim, the Conservative MEP for the North West, part of a delegation of European parliamentarians, who was hiding in the basement of the hotel. He told Sky News: 'I was in the lobby of the hotel when the gunmen came in and people started running. There were about 25 or 30 of us… a gunman just stood there spraying bullets around, right next to me.'

Another family friend, who was a policeman, gave Irene the UK Foreign and Commonwealth Office number in London. Irene dialled and was told that a helpline was being set up, and would be available after 9pm. Lynne said the bank would send her a mobile phone and a fax machine, but Irene politely declined, saying she wasn't sure she was going to need them.

Lynne phoned every hour right throughout that night. If she was going to be five minutes late, a bank colleague would phone and tell Irene she was slightly delayed. Gradually the house became quieter, with those left watching the TV screen as it repeated the same morsels of news. The remote control was passed around as they channel-surfed between BBC, ITN and Sky, keen for any kind of update.

Irene was frustrated that she still couldn't get through to the Foreign Office's helpline in London. The switchboard was obviously jammed with callers. Then there was a local Grampian Television news bulletin showing Alex Salmond, Scotland's First Minister, speaking in the Scottish Parliament in Edinburgh about the problems with Scotland's banks – and then he referred to the incident in Mumbai.

'That's our local MP,' said Irene.

'Maybe we should contact him,' suggested Karine.

'Why don't we try.'

They thought about it for a moment or two. They shrugged. They weren't sure how to go about it or if it was the right thing.

Unknown to Irene, Alex Salmond was already in frequent contact with RBS, and was being updated about my situation. Most of the family drifted off, as Mary Wilson stayed up with Irene until 5.20am, and then somehow managed to go home, have a shower, and head off to work in the bank.

Karine also stayed the night, and she went out to meet Christopher's works van at 6.30am to tell the foreman Chris wouldn't be going to work for the duration. Irene had them in her 'nest', and she didn't want her brood out of sight in case there was any developing news; this included Lisa, who should have been on her work placement, and Stephanie, who was kept off school.

I tried to switch my mobile devices to silent as there was now a welter of calls and text messages from friends and wellwishers who had no idea about my predicament. I longed to reply.

I could see the numbers and familiar caller-names but I didn't dare speak to anyone unless it was absolutely necessary. I was petrified to make a sound.

I'd wrapped the Blackberry in a towel, still keeping it pressed to my chest. In the pitch black, any spillage of light would have indicated that someone was in the room. And for some reason I couldn't shut off the ring tone on one of my mobiles, so I had to watch it and kill any sounds immediately when a call came in. This all sharpened the extreme stress I was enduring.

Taking flight: Pigeons fly away as the Taj Mahal Palace & Tower Hotel burns during the terror attacks. The day before, Roger Hunt and his colleagues had been dining in the hotel restaurant. © Press Association Images

Under attack: An Indian soldier takes cover as fighting continues between the military and the militants. The siege at the Taj Mahal Hotel was brought to an end after the gun battle, concluding three days of terror in Mumbai during which more than 150 people were killed. © Press Association Images

Running for safety: A soldier runs in front of the Taj Mahal Hotel as the battle between the Indian Black Cat commandos and the terrorists rages inside the hotel corridors and rooms. © Press Association Images

Train station attack: The aftermath of the attacks in Chhatrapati Shivaji railway station, where over 50 people were killed. Just over one hour before the massacre, Bharat, Roger Hunt's hotel driver, invited him to view inside the terminal. Roger declined. © Press Association Images

Headline news: An Indian newspaper reports the attacks on the front page. The violence made headlines across the world. © Press Association Images

Gateway of India: The Taj Mahal Hotel and the Gateway of India monument. The terrorists reached the hotel by docking in the harbour. © Shutterstock

Tribute to the fallen: Indians light candles at a memorial in Chhatrapati Shivaji station to the victims of the attacks following the guilty verdict in the trial of the sole surviving gunman in the 2008 terror attacks, Pakistani Mohammed Ajmal Kasab. © Press Association Images

Memorial candles: Mumbai residents light candles in tribute to the victims of the attacks in November 2010. © Press Association Images

Happier memories: Roger Hunt as a little boy (right) photographed at a family wedding in Edinburgh in 1974, with his mum and dad, brothers Raymond and Christopher and sister Lynne.

Brothers together: An early picture (with Roger Hunt on the right) taken with his brothers Raymond and Christopher.

Aberdeenshire days: A primary school photograph with Roger Hunt in the middle. This was a picture Roger recalled during his darker moments under siege in Room 1478. It reminded him of growing up in Whitehills, on the Banffshire coast, and going to Pittodrie stadium with his brothers to watch Aberdeen FC in the 1980s.

In memory of those lost at sea: The commemorative plaque which hangs in the Fishermens' Mission in Kinlochbervie, in Sutherland, Scotland, as a tribute to the crew of the MB *Bon Ami* BF 323. Roger's brother Christopher was among those who died.

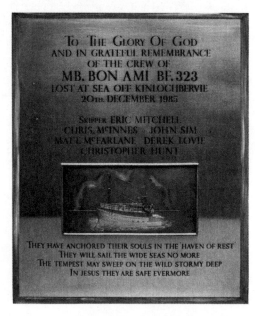

Finding his anchor: A wedding picture of Roger Hunt with his wife Irene on their wedding day on 8 August 1987. The picture is taken on the hill overlooking the harbour in Macduff, once one of Scotland's busiest fishing ports.

All together again: Roger Hunt, Irene, Lisa, Christopher and Stephanie, at a family wedding shortly after his return home to Macduff. During several of his darkest moments in Mumbai, Roger believed he was going to die and that he would never again enjoy such a happy family moment.

Focus on the future: Roger Hunt's children, Lisa, Christopher and Stephanie. Much of his time lying in darkness on the Oberoi hotel room floor was spent thinking about his children. It was his sense of pride in them all that sparked his acute sense of survival.

CHAPTER FOURTEEN

Slaughter at My Door

I HAD BEEN lying behind the couch for some time. It was nearly midnight and it had all gone rather quiet. I was beginning to make out the shapes in the room again, at least the smoke was clearing.

Outside in the street the crowds had obviously been pushed back out of harm's way. The sirens and the traffic had died down. I began to think that perhaps I might steal a look outside the door and survey the situation. I was close to making a move, but again I stopped and listened. I decided to give myself another 15 minutes before opening my door; meanwhile you could have heard a pin drop.

Elsewhere in the hotel the terrorists were still in control. Amid all the confusion they had rounded up a number of hostages from the restaurants. Around a dozen people were herded into the kitchen of the Tiffin, and then taken up the stairs. Eyewitness Seyfi Muezzinoglu, a Turkish businessman, and his wife, Meltem, were among this group. They were the only survivors.

Seyfi later told a Channel Four's *Dispatches* documentary: 'Some tried to escape and were shot down mercilessly. The one in black went up the stairs and said: "All the women up." And all the women went up the stairs.'

Seyfi was with the other men on the landing. 'All of a

sudden, he raises his gun and at that moment my wife screamed out: 'Stop, stop. He's from Turkey. He's a Muslim'.'

The gunman made a gesture for Seyfi to throw himself down on the ground – which he did immediately. Then the captor opened fire again, shooting more victims who crumpled in a bloody heap, with Seyfi buried under their bodies. The weeping and screaming women were forced to step over the bodies and were ordered to make their way up the stairs. Seyfi was told to stand up and join the women.

In my room I was contemplating making a break for it, down the very same stairs that the terrorists and their hostages were heading up. After ten minutes I began to hear doors clicking. Clearly other guests had the same idea of tentatively stepping out into the corridor. Perhaps people were thinking it was now all clear and the terrorists had moved on; maybe they knew something I didn't. But I was shaken to the core when I heard a door hinge creak open and then a wailing shriek from a woman.

'Arrrrrrrrr! No, no, no!'

Then there was the familiar sound of those dreadful machine guns.

DRRRRRRRRRRRRR!

DRRRRRRRRR! DRRRRRRRRR!

There followed a heart-wrenching moan of pain, a primal cry like a wounded animal groaning with its last breath.

And then silence once again.

This poor, unknown woman must certainly be dead, I thought. This was a severe blow for me – there was no way I would be leaving shortly. Moments later the shock and awe continued as more grenades exploded, and I scurried back to my shelter behind the couch. I crouched down and started to fire emails back to Edinburgh saying that the terrorists were still in control.

I knew that my Blackberry inbox was filling up with extra mail – so I needed someone to clear them all out. At least when I looked at the charging icon I could see that there was plenty left. I was thankful that I'd kept it on charge most of the time in Mumbai: a lesson that has been passed on for future trips.

From: Lesley Laird
Sent: Wednesday 26 November 18:20
To: Roger Hunt
Subject: We are getting your mailbox emptied so you can reply to us.

From: Lorraine Kneebone
Sent: Wednesday 26 November 18:22
To: Roger Hunt
Subject: RE: Hello
Jesus Christ Rog. Hold in there. We are alerting every-body here we can possibly think of. I am praying you are OK. Is there any way to get away... are you ok at the mo?

From: Lorraine Kneebone
Sent: Wednesday 26 November 18:26
To: Roger Hunt
Subject: RE: Hello
Hi Rog We are on phone right now to IT services getting your inbox size increased in case you can't mail us cause it is full. It may take a wee while. Please email us if at all possible, even a couple of words...

I was still shocked to the core by the murder of the person outside the door. There were longer periods of inactivity in the Oberoi and the surrounding area but I could hear sporadic gun battles going on elsewhere in the vicinity.

I was completely unaware of the fact that the attackers had fanned out across the city and other places in Mumbai had been targeted. The first few hours were utter chaos for the police. Dozens of innocent Indians were caught up in the terror, and many brave policemen, including Ashok Kamte the police commissioner, and Vijay Salaskar, an inspector, lost their lives in an ambush near the hospital in the early hours. Hemant Karkare, the head of the anti-terrorist forces, was killed in the Taj Mahal.

Behind my couch I had no notion of the wider situation.

Looking back, if there was anything that might have been done for me, it would have been to have been kept updated about the bigger picture. I understand why this wasn't possible. The security services had recommended to my bank colleagues that I be given only information that was personal or key for me to stay alive. It was important that nothing else slipped into the hands of the killers, who were also using Blackberrys and mobile phone devices to coordinate their attacks. I had vivid fears about what might be going on – but still no sense that this was a terrorist assault. What I later learned was the terrorists were systematically clearing out rooms, looking for Brits and Americans, rounding up hostages and moving them around the hotel.

The murder of innocent people was still going on.

CHAPTER FIFTEEN

Dead or Alive?

EVEN THE GREATEST generals talk about the confusion of battle. Victory is won by those who take the most decisive actions based on the best information available at that time. In the early hours there appears to have been a fog of confusion in India. Initially, this small band of suicidal terrorists had the upper hand, using the element of surprise.

Back in Gogarburn, it was difficult for the bank's security people to get a clear picture of what was happening. The bank was only one of dozens of businesses putting in place operations to get their people back home safely. Lynne and her team were straining to find out what was actually happening in real time. RBS was only one part of the jigsaw and couldn't – and would never have wanted to – interfere in the operations in India.

For Lynne, there were some basic aims: keeping me focused on staying alive and making sure there was a flow of relevant information to Irene back in Macduff.

From: Lesley Laird
Sent: Wednesday 26 November 18:40
To: Roger Hunt
Subject: Mailbox getting cleared now! Keep strong we're all still here

From: Lesley Laird
Sent: Wednesday 26 November 18:49
To: Roger Hunt
Subject: Still working with GT [Group Technology]
– *nearly there now...*

From: Lesley Laird
Sent: Wednesday 26 November 19:01
To: Roger Hunt
Subject: RE: R U OK???
OK Rog. I'm at my pc if you want to keep emailing.

From: Lesley Laird
Sent: Wednesday 26 November 19:02
To: Roger Hunt
Subject: Are you getting this – are you ok – Please email
if you can

From: Lesley Laird
Sent: Wednesday 26 November 19:06
To: Roger Hunt
Subject: Your mail box has been expanded – you can
send emails.

From: Lesley Laird
Sent: Wednesday 26 November 19:23
To: Roger Hunt
Subject: Are you safe?

From Stan Hosie
Sent: Wednesday 26 November 19:16
To: Roger Hunt
Subject: Please reply if possible

I hadn't closed my eyes all night. I'd been awake, although
I was floating from one dreamlike state to another. My

thoughts kept drifting to Irene. How was she doing? What was she thinking? I knew she was great at coping, it has always been her forte, but this was a terrible situation. What about the kids? How were they bearing up? As I lay there, feeling sore, tired and filthy, I knew I had to try and put this out of my mind. Thinking about my ordinary family life was ripping me apart. I wanted to refocus all of my concentration on what I might be able to do to get myself out of this situation.

During the early hours of Thursday morning there was very little sound. It was all rather eerie. The streets were silent. There was no buzzing of traffic. Away in the far distance I could make out the occasional car hooter. I was tightly tucked in behind the couch, curled in a foetal position, and could feel a small, protruding concrete hook under the carpet. I felt dirty and grubby, the stench of smoke clung to my shirt and my jeans were caked in sticky soot. I had remained awake all night, fully alert in a state of hyper-awareness, my brain racing with so many different fears and worries.

I kept reminding myself: *Roger, stay alert. Keep focused.* But my mind would wander, with my thoughts straying across continents back to Macduff, to Irene, the family and our friends. Only afterwards did I understand that at 3.53am one of the terrorists received a call on his mobile which was monitored by the secret services, and became part of an official transcript. The leader of the operation wanted to find out how the mission was going – and they were in a room beneath me.

'Brother Abdul, the media is comparing your actions to 9/11. One senior police officer has been killed.'

'We are on the 10th and 11th floors. We have five hostages.'

Another voice came on the phone to the terrorists.

'Everything is being recorded by the media. Inflict the maximum damage. Keep fighting. Don't be taken alive.'

The original caller came back on the line.

'Kill all hostages, except the two Muslims. Keep your phone switched on so we can hear the gunfire.'

'We have three foreigners, including women. From Singapore and China,' came the reply.

'Kill them,' they were instructed.

In the recording the terrorists can be heard ordering the hostages to stand in a straight line. There is the sound of gunfire as the hostages are killed, then cheering on the line.

Since the attacks, the ordeal of the Turkish survivors, Seyfi and Meltem Muezzinoglu, has been revealed in detail in the documentary *Secrets of the Dead*, made by PBS. As mentioned above, the couple were among the five hostages taken up the back stairs to the 10th floor. Meltem had the foresight to throw her pashmina over her head. They were taken into a room and lined up with the others for execution, with Seyfi and Meltem pleading with the killers that they were Muslims. The gunmen had already allowed him to live when the men were massacred on the landing, but now Seyfi was asked to prove he was a Muslim. So he recited an Arabic prayer, which convinced the killers to leave them alone. The others were less fortunate.

'I closed my eyes. There was so much shooting,' said Meltem in a harrowing interview.

'The older Indian woman, she didn't fall down. She was standing and smiling. It was rather annoying for them. And she was smiling and looking at us, you know, after having received so many bullets, so the guy put another cartridge in his gun and shot them again,' said her husband.

'When everything stopped, I opened my eyes... the Singapore girl who was holding my hand a few minutes before... I knew she was dead. So I said to my husband, "If we're going to die anyhow, let's pray for the dead."'

And the couple stepped forward, opened their hands and recited an Arabic prayer for the dead. The killers, looked on in wide-eyed disbelief.

The terrorists were then ordered by mobile phone to move on through the hotel – and they left the couple in the room.

Just before the Mumbai sun began to heat another day, the mocking cackle of the crows reached a crescendo. It seemed as if there was a squadron of birds, diving and then soaring in complete contempt of our human frailties. The minutes turned into hours and there was still no concrete sign of my release. Normally one welcomes the daylight, but this dawn brought fresh dangers for me. It left me feeling exposed and vulnerable. I longed for the daylight to disappear and for darkness to shroud my hiding place again. I felt like a sitting duck for the terrorists and this increased my anxiety, so I lay there as quietly as possible.

Then, after nearly ten hours on the floor, there was a ringing in my room.

Drrnngg! Drrnngg! Drrnngg!

What was that?

I was thoroughly startled.

It was the bedside room phone. My impulse was to pick it up to stop the ringing; then I checked myself.

What if this was the terrorists checking on whether the room was occupied? It was an easy way for them to find out who was still stranded in their room.

Drrnngg! Drrnngg! Drrnngg!

Then it stopped.

Despite the clammy heat, I shivered. The six rings had felt like an eternity. I was stirred into action. I emailed Lynne and a Metropolitan Police adviser to find out if anyone was trying to contact me. They said they didn't know. It was my decision whether to answer. For me, this was a life-or-death decision. I chose not to take the call. It is difficult to conclude for certain, but the probability is that this 50–50 decision saved my life.

I was able to send off another email for Stan Hosie.

From: Roger Hunt
Sent: Thursday 27 November 06:19
To: Stan Hosie
Subject: Re: Please reply if possible
What is happening stan. Still tapped ijn hotel

This tiny message was snatched with some relief in Gogarburn. At last there was an indication that I was at least alive. But there was no doubting that I remained in grave peril.

From: Gavin Reid
Sent: Thursday 27 November 06:40
To: Roger Hunt
Subject: Re: Any update
Roger, so glad to hear from you!!!! Firstly, are you ok and what's your status? Still police action to get situation under control roger. Pockets of people in hotel safe so I'm hoping your either still in your room and keeping low or with other people. Please let me know asap. We are here for you roger and can only imagine what you're going through. When we get you out we'll get everything sorted re flights etc.
Gavin

I was so pleased to get this note. I hadn't heard from him for some time. After my earlier phone call to Gavin from my smoking hotel room, he had passed on my whereabouts to

RBS's disaster recovery team in Edinburgh. While he remained extremely worried, he had other pressing staff matters to deal with locally and he felt Lynne and the team in Gogarburn were best placed to coordinate contact with me. He watched the local Mumbai television channels – which were more graphic and immediate than the sanitised BBC and Sky News reports. He was watching the attacks as they unfolded and had heard that the terrorists were scouring for British and American passport holders. He was advised by security to stay put. Mahesh was a popular place with Westerners and a possible target for the terrorists. He had hidden in the basement of the restaurant along with fellow dinners and the staff as the battles raged outside. I fired back a response:

From: Roger Hunt
Sent: Thursday 27 November 06:42
To: Gavin Reid
Subject: RE: Any update
Alone in my room. When are police coming.

From: Gavin Reid
Sent: Thursday 27 November 07:16
To: Roger Hunt
Subject: RE: Any update
Roger, this must be really hard but you need to sit tight. I've updated Lynne so we're all relieved to hear from you but still very concerned. Please keep the communication up if you can and that will be between me, you and Lynne.
As soon as we get you out I'm going to do my utmost to be there asap and that I can only hope is soon. As tough as it must be you've done the absolute right thing by continuing to sit this out.
Keep communicating...

Hang in there.

Gavin

Hang in there! Hang in there! I was hanging in. Just. But I still had no idea what was actually happening. Then the room phone rang once more.

Drrng! Drnng! Drnng!

Drnng! Drrng! Drnng! Drnng! Drnng!

It was more persistent this time, as if the caller suspected someone was in the room and not answering. I shuddered. And then, thankfully, it stopped.

From: Lynne Highway
Sent: Thursday 27 November 07:24
To: Roger Hunt
Subject: RE: Any update
Hi Rog
We are all so pleased to hear from you. I'm in hourly contact with Irene and she's holding up well – you should be very proud of her. Hang on in there – we're doing everything we can to get you out.
L X L

Back in RBS, the security team were figuring out my options. My brain was working overtime too. If they were confident I would be rescued soon, surely they would have been much quicker and more positive in their response? Something wasn't right – what did they know that they simply couldn't tell me?

From: Stan Hosie
Sent: Thursday 27 November 07:35
To: Roger Hunt
Subject: RE: Please reply if possible
For security reason, please confirm you wife's Christian

name. I will follow your reply with an update.

From: Roger Hunt
Sent: Thursday 27 November 09:13
To: Stan Hosie
Subject: RE: Please reply if possible
Irene

Then there was a nearby explosion which shook the door. It frightened the life out of me after hours of inactivity. I could tell that this was a grenade explosion. It was now about 2pm, local time. There were several more grenades in quick succession, then some more automatic machine gun fire. The terrorists were back. It sounded as if the battle was on the 14th floor. It was getting closer all the time.

From: Roger Hunt
Sent: Thursday 27 November 09:14
To: Lynne Highway
Subject: RE: Any update
They are back in the hotel throwing grenades. I think this is it lynne!

CHAPTER SIXTEEN

Stalked by Fear

MY THOUGHTS HAD been that the longer the silence, the more chance that the gunmen had either been overrun or moved on. Now I was scared. Very scared. They must have regrouped and were back to finish off the job. There was a new development that began to concern me too. There were more gunshots in the street, and coming right into the hotel. It was getting very close.

Drrrrrr! Drrrrrr! Drrrrrrr!

Then single shots like a pop-gun.

Pop! Pop! Pop!

These bullets were hitting the building close to my window. Then there was the shattering of broken glass coming from the floor above. In reply, I could make out the outgoing response.

Drrrrrr! Drrrrrr! Drrrr!

Drrrrrrr! Drrrrr! Drrrrr!

From along the corridors inside the hotel, there was a cacophony of gunfire. My fear had moved into a phase of gnawing desperation and confusion. I was trying to pinpoint exactly where the gunfire might be coming from but ringing ricochets made it difficult.

From: Lynne Highway

Sent: Thursday 27 November 09:26
To: Roger Hunt
Subject: RE: Any update
Rog,
We are doing everything that we can. Hang on in there
– look at what you've already come through – everyone
is thinking about you.
Keep e-mailing and I'll feed into all the team that are
working on this back here.
L XX Lynne

This gun battle went on much of that afternoon. The percussive crump of grenades echoed up from below and more *pop! pop! pop!* gunfire from various directions. I lay still.

Then there was a lull. I started to raise my head.

But I dropped it down again immediately when I heard another small salvo of gunfire slightly further away. I imagined that the army and special forces were moving in on a group of well armed, well organised terrorists, who were shifting from room to room. I couldn't make out if it was friendly fire, or terrorists returning fire on the police. It was all too confusing.

I'd now made up my mind that I was not going to leave the room. Not under these circumstances. So far, my strategy of staying silent was working. I had to continue with it; to stay hidden in the room and hope that the authorities got to me before the terrorists did. I lay behind the couch trying to work out my odds: was it 50-50? Surely not, my chances must be better than that.

Then I would become worried again as another grenade reverberated nearby and the prospect of the door being blown off its hinges troubled my imagination. I had to stay positive;

dwelling on all these awful 'what-ifs' was not going to help me. But the agony went on.

While I'm a fairly fit person who has been active as a runner and footballer, I wasn't cut out for long periods lying on a hard floor in one position. My body was becoming very uncomfortable. I was pressed into this confined space, and my legs, arms and neck were beginning to hurt. My hips and elbows, without any extra padding, were becoming very painful. After years of playing five-a-side football, I began to feel that old knee injury taking its toll. I tried to support my head with my arms for a while, but my elbow dug into the ground. I wriggled around to relieve the aching and the cramp, but there was very little room.

My survival technique was to be as quiet as possible. I also had to stay awake: I knew that I had a tendency to snore. With the curtains and net blinds still closed, the room remained in darkness. I was careful not to make a sound. So if I moved it was very slow, taking my time to turn around. There was increasing discomfiture in my mental state.

Why was it taking the authorities so long to gain control? Surely the Black Cat Commandos could take charge of this urgent situation? This was a question that perplexed the Indian authorities in the aftermath.

I've watched plenty of television series where I've seen the SAS team deployed as a rapid-reaction force. So why was it taking an age? I later learned that the slow response was due to the size and scale of India. The Black Cat Commandos are based south of Delhi and don't have any transport aircraft of their own. The only plane that was available to transport the 200 commandos to Mumbai was a Russian Il-76 transport carrier. This was in Chandigarh, which is 165 miles north of Delhi. The pilot had to be awakened, a crew assembled and the plane fuelled. The aircraft didn't reach Delhi until five hours after the attacks began and it then took another four hours to reach Mumbai. So it was a full ten hours before India's elite force reached Mumbai – and only then were they able to start assessing the situation.

Back in Macduff, there was another matter that Irene had to deal with – the press were now at our door. The news was out that a 'Scottish banker was caught up in the attacks'. It didn't take the press long to pin down my name; but one of the family made the mistake of speaking to an Aberdeen evening newspaper reporter and that simply kindled interest. Then the local correspondent of the *Banffshire Journal* came to the door: he was polite and friendly but Irene declined to comment.

This led to a stream of press people from the *Daily Record*, *The Sun* and other UK tabloids knocking on our door for an interview. They were mainly polite, yet persistent. There was even a local television and radio van parked outside with reporters looking for a comment. Irene had an audio call with Lynne and the RBS's head of media Carolyn McAdam, and the stance was to say nothing rather than risk jeopardising my safe return. In any case, Irene was extremely nervous about talking to the press, so RBS dispatched a media adviser, Ian Elliot, to keep the media at bay and deal with any inquiries. Our home is several feet above the street and difficult to look into, but the family kept the curtains closed to deter prying photographers. A local policeman was sent along to keep watch on the house.

Irene hadn't been to bed. She had been up all Wednesday night, watching and waiting. She had a sixth sense that she would know how I was and, increasingly, her gut feeling was that I remained in mortal danger. While the state of her nerves meant she would disappear to the toilet and retch from time to time, she was never sick.

The arrival of Ian Elliot at 5.30pm on Thursday night

helped lift spirits. According to Irene he was a godsend, an easy-to-get-along-with person who took away a lot of the strain, dealing with the calls and the local police.

Just after 4pm I sent another email.

From: Roger Hunt
Sent: Thursday 27 November 11:10
To: Lynne Highway
Subject: RE: Any update
Random shooting now

Then came an important message from Lynne. I read it several times and it gave me something new to focus on. Now instead of simply asking about my welfare, the message was different, giving me a coping strategy.

From: Lynne Highway
Sent: Thursday 27 November 11:53
To: Roger Hunt
Subject: RE Any Updates?
Hi Rog
The shots that are being taken are likely to be friendly forces, so hold that thought – it hopefully means that you're getting closer to seeing Irene and the kids. We've been liaising with the police in the UK Rog, to ensure that we keep you safe as that's our number one priority. There are a number of things that we need you to do, and I've listed them below. These reflect the information that we have, so whilst I know that some of them are differ- ent to the approach that we've asked you to take so far, these are the right things to do for the situation now. You know me – always moving the goalposts!
As I said, it is likely that the noises you are hearing are

friendly forces, so if you hear anyone approaching your door, you need to:- ensure that there are no barricades at the door to your room; put the light on; stand in the middle of the room showing that you have absolutely nothing in your hands; comply immediately with any direction they provide.

There are a few other things I need you to do for me. Still giving you work when you're in India! Let me know if you hear anybody in a room nearby. I know that you're on the 14th floor – what room number are you in? Describe what things are close to your room – are there any stairs nearby, are you near a lift, etc? Let me know if you have spoken to anyone recently?

It's great that you're contacting us by email, I'd like you and I to keep in touch on a regular basis (consider it your new SLA) – suggest we email each other every 45 minutes, with this being the first one of those emails. So would be good to get a response from you to this one and then another in 45 minutes. The team in P&A all send their love and Irene and the kids are doing OK – they can't wait to see you (particularly as you've got the infamous Hunt Christmas Lights to put up soon!)

Look forward to hearing back from you – take care of you.

L xsx

This was such a useful response. I grinned to myself at the thought of our Christmas lights. Would I make it home for then? I yelled silently to myself, *I'm in Room 1478.* The time difference and the delay in the emails coming through was obviously causing some confusion about my state. Lynne asked me to start putting times in my email.

From: Roger Hunt

Sent: Thursday 27 November 12:08
To: Lynne Highway
Subject: RE: Any update
5.30 lots of shooting. Room 1478.

Back in Gogarburn this email caused fevered consternation. 'Lots of shooting' – what did that actually mean? Lynne and the team were alarmed. She desperately wanted me to respond. But I couldn't, I was too petrified. I didn't dare switch on the Blackberry in case the light shone out in the dark.

Then Mary McCallum, who works in RBS's group security and fraud at Drummond House, emailed me. She told me I was booked on the 2.40am flight home next morning. The flight was delayed and was now due to depart at 5am.

'If you are able to pick this message up could you please contact someone urgently to advise you are safe.'

I longed to be on that flight. But as the hours ticked by I knew that it would be leaving without me. It also bothered me that perhaps the outside world wasn't fully aware of the gravity of my situation.

From: Lynne Highway
Sent: Thursday 27 November 18:31
To: Roger Hunt
Subject: How are you?
Hi Roger – It's 6:30 here, so by my reckoning, midnight with you. Hope that you are OK and bearing up. Would be great if you could drop me a note to update me on your situation. I've been speaking to Irene every hour and she is obviously keen to know how you are. She and the kids are fine – her dad, sister and cousin have been with them most of the today which has been great. Think more family members were arriving tonight to make sure that they have plenty of company. I'm due to

*speak to her in the next half hour or so, so it would be
great to hear from you before then.*
Take care.

L

XsX

Over the next four or five hours I became increasingly
disorientated. This was the darkest time I have ever experienced
in my life. For long spells I was becoming oblivious to what
was happening in the Oberoi Hotel – or outside. Increasingly,
I was shut away in my own introspection. I thought a great
deal about Irene. I knew she would be coping – but I was
anxious to reach out and just touch her.

I remembered when we first met, at the age of 15. We'd
both attended the same secondary school but it wasn't until I
saw her at a local disco in the town hall at Whitehills that we
got together. It was the time of Culture Club, Bananarama,
Ultravox, Spandau Ballet and all the synthesised sounds of
the New Romantic dance music.

I'd seen her before but tonight Irene was petite and
gorgeous, with brown hair and clear green eyes. She was
wearing a yellow dress and trendy black high-heeled boots.
She smiled radiantly as I approached, rather tentatively.

'Hello, Roger.'

'Hi, fancy a dance?' was my rather lame opening gambit,
as the first thumping bass strains of Duran Duran's *Rio* burst
from the speakers.

'Yeah, that would be fine.'

We didn't say much because the music was so loud but she
nodded when I asked her if she'd like to dance to the next
record. And that was it. We started going out that weekend.
And we got married when I was 21, which is a young age in
comparison to people in the 2010s. Within a year of being

married we had Lisa – really a honeymoon baby. I thought about the birth of all of our children and the trials and tribulations we'd been through together; the difficult time when Mary, Irene's mum, died suddenly. She was a brilliant woman who is still greatly missed.

Banff and Macduff seemed light-years away. I closed my eyes tightly and imagined the individual faces of Lisa, Christopher and Stephanie. This was when I started to think about my youngest brother and his death in the boat disaster: were none of us going to die peacefully of old age in our beds?

I recalled the acres of press publicity and the television and radio coverage in the North East of Scotland about the *Bon Ami*. I imagined a front-page article in our local daily newspaper, the *Press & Journal*, with the headline: 'North East Man Dies in Mumbai Attack'. I thought about the reporter turning up at my mum and dad's door asking them for a comment – and a photo of me in happier times. I pictured their stunned faces.

The *P&J* remains an integral part of the local life but it is famous for its more parochial news coverage. There was even that apocryphal headline when the ss *Titanic* sank on its maiden voyage in April 1912 which read: 'North East Man Drowns At Sea'. I thought all about this.

Were my parents now going to lose their oldest son in dramatic and bloody circumstances that were splayed all over the news channels? Surely this would cause them more anguish and pain.

We take our lives so much for granted. A sense of despair began to creep into my thinking. There was a kind of self-pity that I'd never really experienced before in life. It was a 'Why Me?' question. What had I done that meant that I would come to my end in a hotel massacre, so far away from my birthplace? I battled this thought. But as the minutes and hours ticked by without bringing any positive resolution, my doubts increased and my mood became much bleaker.

Then I had a vivid memory of Lisa on her first day at school in Peterhead. The night before Irene had washed Lisa's long hair and tied curlers into it. Next morning this excited five-year-old came down the stairs with wavy blonde hair, a grey skirt, white socks, her sky-blue blouse and grey cardigan. She had a brand new schoolbag. She looked just lovely. I'd enjoyed watching her grow up, seeing her and being with her at weekends, and then how she headed off to university. I could see a lot of me in her character: her drive, enthusiasm and that Hunt determination; never satisfied unless something was done as perfectly as possible.

My mind flitted to Christopher and to Stephanie. I thought, I will never see them get on as adults, get married, have their own children. Call me an old-fashioned Scotsman in some ways, but the opportunity to walk my girls down the aisle at their weddings is something I wish for. My eyes filled up with big tears; my lungs, throat and mouth were sore and I tried to suppress a cough. All this was cutting me up inside.

I thought of Christopher. Only a few days previously we'd been watching one of our home-made videos. It had made us all laugh. There he was as a toddler, obsessed by his grandad's fishing boats: it was obviously in his blood. His grandad had got him a blue boiler-suit from a local fishing supplies store and tied up a bit of fishing net in the garage. Then Christopher would be given a blunt knife – real fishermen's blades are always sharpened like razors – to pretend to mend the nets. He just looked the part. Then I remembered when I was one of those keen dads looking after the boys' football team when he was playing. There was one particular goal he scored which stuck in my mind; I could see him weaving past two defenders and sweetly chipping the ball over the approaching goalkeeper. I swear it was as good as any goal I'd seen at Pittodrie. I kept thinking how proud I was of him, how hard he worked in his apprenticeship, how he would have to face the burden of being the only man in the family when I perished here. But I had absolute belief that he would look after our family.

More memories of my children flooded into my mind. I'd been at the birth of all three of my children. I thought of 'my baby' Stephanie and how all this would be breaking her heart. Every time I left home she would be the one to give me a cuddle and tell me to drive safely and look after myself. Often when I'd left home on a Sunday evening to start the working week, I'd rummage in my coat pocket for a handkerchief and find a bar of Cadbury's Dairy Milk chocolate – my favourite – which she has secretly placed there.

How would they cope without me? Irene and I had worked all of our lives to give our kids every chance in their lives. I started to calculate what they would have to live on: the death-in-service benefits of my employment at the bank. I knew they would have a roof over their head with the mortgage paid off, but what about the other things in life? There were financial implications too because Lisa was at university.

I also considered the young gunmen who had attacked the hotel. Who were they? Was this al-Qaeda? Was this inspired by Osama bin Laden? Did they really believe in a Jihad holy war against the 'infidels' of the West, or had they been brainwashed with the prospect of glory and a happy hereafter?

From the strength of the attack, the firepower and the time it was taking to regain law and order, I thought they must be a well-armed, well-drilled group. I've been fully aware of the West's 'War on Terror'; of how the UK ended up in support of the United States after the September 11 attack on New York and Washington in 2001. I knew about Tony Blair's wholehearted backing of President Bush and the political fury caused by the so-called 'Weapons of Mass Destruction' which President Saddam Hussein was meant to possess and which took Britain into war in Iraq.

I've been sceptical about the aims, about why we've been dragged into all this conflict, but I've always believed as a citizen you should support your country's democratic decisions, even if they are unpalatable at times. I've constantly admired the men and women of Britain's armed forces and I was humbled now, as I understood my own terror, that they choose to put their lives at risk in the line of fire when confronting global terror. Privately though, I'd questioned why brave and courageous young Scottish soldiers were fighting and dying in Helmand Province in Afghanistan. I imagined the Taliban and the fighting that was going on against British and Allied troops, I thought about the increasing radicalisation of Muslims in the UK, the rising anger at what some saw as an attack on their culture and religion.

I tried to work this all out in my head. Where were the attackers coming from? I guessed they might have connections with some extremist element in Pakistan.

By why target me? A banker from Scotland, trying to create something lasting and worthwhile. I've always believed that commerce and enterprise are the drivers that raise people out of the poverty traps. Capitalism isn't perfect, it has huge flaws, gulfs between the rich and the poor, but it's the best of all the available systems, surely?

All of this senseless killing had nothing to do with me. I'd never raised a word or weapon in anger and had always shown complete respect for other people's cultures and countries.

CHAPTER SEVENTEEN

Back in Touch

MY WEARY COLLEAGUES in Gogarburn were now going through their own rollercoaster of emotions: fear, despondency, frustration, anger and deepening worry. Lying in my daze, I had been out of contact for some time – and they began to presume the worst. As long as I was emailing they knew that I was still alive. But as the television news coverage painted an ever bleaker picture of the scene, hinting at the Indian Army and police's acute difficulty in bringing order back to the city, they began to question my survival. *Has his Blackberry packed in? Has he fallen asleep? Is he unconscious?* These were the 'best' scenarios. Now there were more difficult questions: *Has the fire spread and overcome him? Has he been caught in an explosion?*

At several stages, Lynne and the team thought I was near to death – and that they just couldn't get to me. What was unsaid – and incredibly hard – was that many of my colleagues feared I might have perished: that I was dead. There was an intense personal dimension for Lynne because she had known me for a number of years and the feeling of responsibility hung heavy over her. No one said it out loud, but there was desperation in their faces.

In Macduff, Irene and the gathering were desperate for any kind of news. Lynne was still in touch, and there had been several audio calls where Irene dialled in and heard all of the updates on the activity. Her impression from the news coverage was that the Indian Army was beginning to take control of the situation. There were reports that terrorists had been shot and killed in some of the battles. But the civilian death toll had risen to more than a hundred people. There was still plenty of worry about my safety.

Irene was finding the commotion, the media fuss and the lack of information all highly disconcerting. It was all feeding a sense of almost group hysteria at home. The love and support had been overwhelming. Now everyone was dog-tired and people were clutching at so many what-ifs. So she calmly asked everybody to go home and get some proper rest. Reluctantly they began to drift out of the house – with Irene's dad the last to depart. She made a pact with Lynne that they would both get some rest and speak again in the morning.

Eventually the house was quiet enough for Irene to organise a few things in her mind. It is something she has always been brilliant at doing. She is a fixer, an arranger, a person who copes. It was now nearly 2am. She lay down on our double bed, closed her eyes and began to plan my funeral, in case that was what she was going to be faced with. She knew I wasn't religious and she envisaged a humanist service in the town hall. She would ask Lynne to recommend one of my RBS colleagues to deliver the eulogy. She had some favourite music in mind and she was thinking of a suitable epitaph for my headstone. As she pondered all of this, a few private tears rolled down her cheeks.

At roughly the same time, on the other side of the world, my mind was plumbing even darker depths and I couldn't control it. I was dead. I started to see my own funeral. A piercingly cold Banffshire morning in the graveyard on the outskirts of our town: behind the wall, the rows of solid granite tombstones, neatly tended, and a huddle of people standing before a dark and empty void. I watched the wooden coffin being pulled out of a black motor hearse. I could see Christopher as one of the pall-bearers with the coffin on his shoulder as the burial party moved slowly in step toward the grave. I knew his sturdy spirit and that even at 18 years old he would be able to bear this horrible grief like a young stoical Banffshire man.

All of this was making me feel more desperate. Everything I had achieved in my life would now count for nothing. What if the terrorists were still fixing up this hotel for another almighty explosion? This was unbearable to consider, so I tried to push the thought right out of my head. I began to resent those faceless assailants who were dictating my fate; and I began to think about taking my own life – in my own way.

What were my options? An overdose of tablets, perhaps? But my toilet bag in the bathroom had a packet of headache tablets, that was unlikely to do the job. I had two other options. There was the fruit knife; could I slit my own throat with it? Not really. So would I just get up, open the door, walk out and face the bullets? What would it feel like to have my flesh ripped by bullets and for me to bleed to death in a hotel corridor? It would be quick at least – and the pain would not last long. Strangely enough, I had no fear of this. I knew I was going to die. Not if, but when.

It had been some time since I'd looked at my emails. I hadn't responded to Lynne's email at midnight and I rubbed my eyes and face, trying to shake myself out of my delirious state. I unwrapped the Blackberry from the towel. There were a host of new messages, the names of the people urging and willing me to survive. I simply couldn't let them down.

There were several from Lynne. While her own inner emotional state might have being wrung out, she was ice cool and professional in sticking to her script.

From: Lynne Highway
Sent: Friday 28 November 00:11
To: Roger Hunt
Subject: Yes, it's me again...
You got it, I'm going to keep pestering you by email until we get you back!
If you're reading this, I hope that you're OK and thinking positive thoughts. I know that you've been there a long time now. I can't even begin to imagine how you are feeling and what you are thinking, but I do know that you are incredibly strong and have the inner strength to get through this Rog. You also have great family and friends who are keeping everything crossed for you just now.
Let me know how you are when you can – stay safe and be strong! L xsx

It was nearly 7.15am on Friday morning – I had been on the floor of the room for over 30 hours. My reply was bleary and garbled. But it covered all the basic points.

From Roger Hunt
To: Lynne Highway
Sent: Friday 28 November 01:44
Subject: Re: Yes, it's me again...
7.15. U been heavy gunfire all night. Not sure thry going to get to me in time.

My mood swung back again into survival mode. In all this deep inner darkness, I realised that I desperately wanted to live. I wanted to savour the rest of my life with my wife, family and friends.

Fuck it, Roger, I swore at myself. Get a fuckin' grip of yourself, man. This is NOT where you're going to die. Not here. Not now. You've too much to live for – now is not the time to give up.

From that moment I knew I was going to survive. The circumstances hadn't changed but now my outlook had reversed. My children would not have to live with the thought that I had given up. Somehow I turned my negative, self-pitying thoughts around into a positive drive to live. I had convinced myself that I was going to get out – alive. It was now me against them.

After all, I was from Macduff – and my mate Stuart Anderson reminded me in an email that this meant a lot in life.

From: stuartfaedunfy@aol.com
To: Roger Hunt
Sent: Thursday 27 November 17:41
Subject: Hey buddy
Dogde – Mary keepin me informed but last heard you sent an email so thot id try that!! Is ther nae enuf excitement in your life as it is without getting yourself caught up in this. It shoundnae happen to a boy fae macduff so try n blend in as best only u can?? If you get this ping back and I can try and let abody know your fine (ish) keep your chin up.

Although I longed to reply to his Doric diatribe, I had to keep the Blackberry clear. But looking back, this message really perked me up. The Doric, which is the working-class dialect of the North East and Banffshire, is still such a great treasure trove of humour – and Stuart's note was a real boost.

My early morning email also gave my colleagues back in

Gogarburn a tremendous boost. They knew – after hours of silence – that I was still hanging in. The message was beamed around the all-night team: 'Roger's still alive: he's been in touch.'

CHAPTER EIGHTEEN

Caught in a Gun Battle

MY MOUTH AND TONGUE were as rough as the hull of a bar-nacled trawler. I craved something to drink. This acute sensation of thirst was something I'd never experienced before. I thought of the young girl and her brother at the airport pleading with me for the water I gave them. I had plenty of it then, now I was desperate for just a mouthful.

I'd stuck with my decision not to use the minibar – I'd had nothing to drink since Wednesday evening, and it was nearly 35 hours since the attack. I knew there was a half litre bottle of water in the fridge. It was increasingly tempting. But I couldn't risk making a move. I felt giddy and delirious. It was quiet and outside the crows were circling around and cackling once again.

I heard helicopters overhead during the night. The sound of the rotor-blades increased in intensity, coming very near to the hotel. This was an encouraging sign. I had visions of an SAS-style attack, with the special forces landing on the roof, and abseiling down the side of the building. I was a teenager when the SAS stormed the Iranian embassy in London in 1980. It was an amazing tale of British derring-do. Now I thought a swoop would lead to my rescue, through the window. But the helicopters droned away off into the distance. It never occurred to me that the commandos were being dropped onto the hotel roof after sliding down a rope from the aircraft.

A huge gun battle broke out on the Friday morning with a terrifying screech of bullets and the deafening thud of rocked-propelled shells and grenades flying through the air and crumping into the concrete walls outside.

The response was a flurry of machine gun fire from a position above my room.

Drrrrrr! Drrrrr! Drrrr!

Pop. Pop. Pop.

Drrrrrrrrr. Drrrrrrrrr. Drrrrrrrr!

Glass was shattering, the dust in the room was kicked up off the floor, the crashing and cracking of concrete was going on around me. With gunfire outside and above me, I knew a battle was raging. I curled up even tighter in my human ball, my ears ringing with the shock waves.

It was then that I actually contemplated the existence of a great and forgiving God. Was there a Christian God or a Muslim Allah who was right? Was there really a supreme being allowing all this carnage to go on? What was it that spurred on the terrorists – to take on a suicidal battle they could not hope to win for what they saw as a 'just' cause?

My own upbringing was through connections with the Church of Scotland and I understood the differences with the Roman Catholic church. In the North East of Scotland there are Methodists, Seventh-day Adventists, Episcopalians and Baptists: all branches of the Christian faith. But since the death of my brother I had been an avowed atheist, someone who did not believe in the existence of any god – Christian, Muslim, Sikh or Hindu. I looked at life in a much more pragmatic and humanist way, removed from the spiritual world. I thought about my brother standing on the bridge of the trawler waiting in vain to be rescued in those high seas. Surely if there was a gracious God, He would have intervened.

I became increasingly traumatised. The gunfire was intense and continued for several hours. The room was reverberating. I thought about compromising my beliefs and praying to God: asking Him to help me, and keep me safe. Somehow I thought this would make me a hypocrite, only asking for help when I was under extreme duress. No, if I was going to find a way out this, it would be through the love and support of my family back home. It would be through my positive desire to live and looking for every opportunity to stay alive.

Another grenade exploded above. Then there was a salvo of gunfire. It was all very frightening. I began to wonder if the building could stand such a sustained battering. The foundations were shuddering. I started to think the whole edifice might collapse and I'd be buried under tonnes of concrete and steel wreckage.

There were more single pistol shots, then machine gun fire and more grenades. I imagined this was the terrorists forcing their way into rooms, then killing the occupants. Each spray of gunfire was getting closer. When was my time coming? How long could this go on? I listened more closely: yes, there were exchanges of fire too. Could this mean the military or the police were winning ground? I didn't know this, but the increasing intensity was an indication that the Black Cat Commandos had finally arrived and were now engaged in retaking the hotel, floor by floor, room by room.

Back in the Gogarburn hothouse, the polystyrene coffee cups were piling up and there were a few weary faces, but people were still working with every ounce of energy to keep me going. Most had been in the office for over 40 hours without leaving – but their spirits had been raised by the email I'd sent. Lynne was exhausted, so she was encouraged to head over to RBS's Business School for a few hours' sleep.

She passed over her duties to Andrew Sharman, whom I had met briefly. He would be the points person throughout the night, with the strict proviso that if anything major developed Lynne was to be awakened immediately. The Business School is only three minutes walk from the main RBS building.

Andrew's job in the bank is Safety, Health and Wellbeing Manager. And this was a crisis of safety, health and wellbeing at its most acute. Andrew now took on a dominant role in keeping me focused. And alive. His trail of cajoling emails gave me something fresh to think about. Andrew's persistence and ability to keep me motivated also showed the calibre of so many of my colleagues and their ability to rally round and work as a team.

His first email came from the address of the wonderfully-named Chanel Rock, who is a Risk Manager in the bank. Andrew wanted me to respond to Chanel's email because back in Gogarburn an automatic 'Out of Office' reply had bounced back from my Blackberry. That wasn't helpful. Andrew simply wanted me to click back a manual response. Even a blank one would let them know I was still there.

From: Chanel Rock
Sent: Friday 28 November 01:55
To: Roger Hunt
Subject: URGENT PRIORITY Simple emails Roger as quickly as you can. Am sitting at the PC and will await your confirmation. We are in constant contact with Lynne on your behalf. Sit tight friend, we are all with you here.

From: Chanel Rock
Sent: Friday 28 November 03:32
To: Roger Hunt
Subject: URGENT PRIORITY
Roger

REPLY TO THE FOLLOWING PLEASE:
- ** DO YOU HAVE BLACKBERRY CHARGER?*
- ** DO YOU HAVE POWER?*
- *Stick in mate, help is on its way, you're doing a great job.*
- *I'm looking forward to seeing you soon.*
- *Andrew*

Andrew pestered and pestered. Every 15 minutes there was another message in the Inbox. At 4:15am UK time he urged me to '*email to acknowledge receipt of this message – and to hang in there buddy*'. Then at 4:43am he fired another URGENT – READ IMMEDIATELY. He informed me that things were beginning to happen and he gave me some essential instructions: do not barricade the door; have nothing in your hands; comply immediately with directions given.

He went on... after another 15 minutes... with his Golden Rules. He told me he was sitting in House A with a roomful of colleagues all rooting for me. They had been in the office since Wednesday morning. Nearly two full days. What wonderful devotion! At 5.56am he pinged yet another: Are you remembering the Rules?

Hello mate Sorry to bother you again, just want to ensure that you are thinking of my Rules!! He signed off with: *Stick in mate, reckon we'll both be needing a beer when you get home!*

From: Roger Hunt
To: Chanel Rock
Sent: Friday 28 November 2008 06:25
Subject: Re: Are you remembering the Rules?
When though. 3 days without food drink or sleep starting to tell

In RBS's Meeting Room N1/1 there was another high-powered audio conference call with senior security officials in London. The Metropolitan Police told Lynne and Andrew that a local police officer called Dave Astill would be making contact with me. They were to send me an identification code so that I would know it was him. Yet somehow, in all the fury and noise of the gunfire, I missed this vital email message – and the code.

In my defence, I was pretty shell-shocked. Then, horror of horrors, I saw my Blackberry flashing with *INCOMING CALL*. I gulped. My Blackberry wasn't supposed to take calls – the bank doesn't enable them for calls! But it was flashing and flashing. For a split second I wondered if I should answer. What if it was the terrorists? But then logic kicked in and I realised that someone back in Gogarburn has probably changed the settings.

'Hello,' I said tentatively.

'Hi, Roger. It's Dave here. What room are you in?'

'Eh, what?'

'Look, Roger, I'm a hostage negotiator with the Met Police and I'm in Mumbai. What's your room number?'

'Sorry, I don't know you – where's Lynne?' I asked suspiciously.

'Didn't you get the code message?'

'What code message?' I blurted out, becoming rather agitated. 'If you are who you say you are, you will know my room number!'

'OK, OK, calm down. I'll sort this out and someone will get back to you. But Roger, we're doing all we can to get you out safely.'

The phone went dead. I lay there replaying it all in my head. Code message? Who was Dave? Why was he phoning me on my Blackberry? Then Andrew's email gave me the answer and a renewed sense of hope.

From: Chanel Rock
Sent: Friday 28 November 07:27
To: Roger Hunt
Subject: You're a STAR!
Hello mate
I understand that you have been speaking to the Police
– great work! Just wanted to let you know I haven't for-
gotten about you, just giving some space to let Police
contact you. What kind of beer do you fancy when you
get back? I'll get them ready up at the Bistro. Can't wait
to see you pal.
Andrew
PS – Now don't forget the Rules!!
DO NOT BARRICADE YOUR DOOR
HAVE NOTHING IN YOUR HANDS
COMPLY IMMEDIATELY WITH DIRECTIONS GIVEN
Andrew

So the police were trying to get in contact. That was
heartening. But Andrew's instructions were paramount. I
read them again and again to get them into my head.

From: Roger Hunt
Sent: Friday 28 November 07:31
To: Andrew Sharman
Subject: RE: You're a STAR!
Not out yet so still don't feel safe. Will need something a
little stronger than beer.

From: Andrew Sharman
To: Roger Hunt
Sent: Friday 28 November 2008 07:32
Subject: RE: You're a STAR
Yes, but I didn't say it would be only a pint. I'm planning

a much bigger session for us mate! We are on another conf call now, making good progress, hang in buddy, we are getting close. Are you a whisky or vodka man?

There were more emails about the rules I needed to follow. Then Andrew played a cute game with me. He said I'd get a pint of beer – at least I thought it was beer – for every rule I sent back correctly. Never one to give up on some free pints, I replied:

Don't Barricade door; Say have nothing in my hands; follow every instruction.

Andrew responded:

Don't know whether to be smiling or not, that just cost me 3 pints!!!!!, Good work fella, we are all smiling here – you're a hero mate, stick in, hold tight.

The Blackberry was continuing to be my lifesaver. Andrew was doggedly persistent: and his next email signed-off: '*Almost there buddy, hold tight, stay safe and remember the Rules!*' But I began to worry that it was running out of juice. Andrew was obviously concerned too. It was just 8.05am in Edinburgh when he raised the question.

Rog, How's your Blackberry doing? How many 'bars' of charge do you have there? Are you able to keep it plugged in and charged up? Let me know matey please, Andrew.

My arms were stiff and sore now. Typing was becoming more difficult. It took me a few minutes to respond. I could see the charger on the bureau but the gunfire was so heavy I wasn't going to risk blowing my cover.

From: Roger Hunt
To: Andrew Sharman

Sent: Friday 28 November 08:09
Subject: Re: Your Blackberry
3 bars and cannot charge.

The email exchange with Andrew was keeping my mind off a lot of more pressing matters: there was still gunfire going on. He responded to my news about the Blackberry.

Thanks mate, that's good news. 3 bars is plenty of juice. Won't be long now Rog, you're doing an absolutely amazing job there. Have you suffered an injuries, or just hungry, tired and thirsty? Keep thinking about those beers – think I'm due you 4 so far – that right?
Andrew.

The thought of a cold drink was a fresh torture. I struggled to get my fingers onto the tiny keyboard. But replied:

Sore lungs from skohe inhalation first night.

Just before 9am, there was another email from Andrew.

Hi Rog Can you give me a quick update on what's happening there please mate? Ohh, and don't forget my 'Rules'. DO NOT BARRICADE YOUR DOOR, HAVE NOTHING IN YOUR HANDS; COMPLY IMMEDIATELY WIH DIRECTIONS GIVEN.

I was again angling my body into position to reply, when there was another blast which shook me.

Still in room no sign of help and a grenade has just exploded.

Andrew tried to reassure me.

I understand that the explosion there just now was a stun grenade going off as police are clearing the floors. Hang in buddy, stay strong, and safe and stick to the Rules.

I repeated the rules to myself again: DO NOT BARRICADE YOUR DOOR. HAVE NOTHING IN YOUR HANDS. COMPLY IMMEDIATELY WITH DIRECTIONS GIVEN. Then Andrew said something that I cherished:

I will not leave until you are safe.

It was a kind thing to say.

CHAPTER NINETEEN

Life or Death at Gunpoint

I HAD BEEN TOLD clearly what to do. There was no quibble about that. All my life I have known the importance of following instructions. It's been part of my job to communicate what people must do in certain critical situations. Nothing could be clearer. I trusted Andrew Sharman with my life. He had given me 'The Rules' – I repeated them back to him:

DO NOT BARRICADE YOUR DOOR: COMPLY IMMEDIATE-LY WITH DIRECTIONS GIVEN... AND HAVE NOTHING IN YOUR HANDS.

And yet... and yet. I had been told that my release would be soon. But then I heard a violent crash in the room next door. I'd seen my neighbour disappear into his room at the outset, when he thought all the commotion was celebratory firecrackers. I sat up and strained my ears. I could make out muffled shouts.

I heard an instruction being barked and another voice cry out. This sounded more like the terrorists at his door, rather than rescue forces. That was my assessment. I held my breath again, waiting for the gun shots. My worst fear was that, despite the intense gun battles, the armed forces had not been able to gain the upper hand, and the terrorists still controlled the hotel. But there was no gunfire. For 15 minutes I listened.

I was rigid and in a state of hyper-alertness. Then I heard scuffling right outside my door. My heart was pounding. This was it for me. I took a deep breath. This was the moment of life – or death.

I'd followed the first rule: the door wasn't barricaded.

I was lying still crouched on my right hand side, bracing myself. My arm and side were completely numb and I couldn't move. It was now painful... but the adrenalin overcame any injury as I heard the activity right outside my door.

I had the small knife in my hand. I gripped the handle tightly, bracing myself for the last-ditch moment when I might have to fight for my life.

'Open the door! Open the door!' came the command.

So what did I do?

I had also been told to stand up with my arms raised. I'd played the game with Andrew Sharman over and over again. For goodness sake, he owed me a few cold beers on that score. But immediately a sense of survival overruled this basic instruction. *What if this is the terrorists?* By standing up I was going to give them an easy target to kill me.

The crash on the door was terrific as it caved in. I didn't dare look over the couch. The heavy footsteps swept into the room, and there was the clicking of metallic weapons.

Then light began to invade my refuge.

I knew it. I had done the wrong thing – being hidden made me a suspicious target for the Black Cats.

'Please don't shoot!... Please don't shoot!' I pleaded.

I remember seeing the black metallic barrel of a gun come prodding over the top of the couch. I dropped the knife and slide it under the couch. I tried to pull myself up – but my right arm was too numb. I scanned the three men. I couldn't distinguish them from the gunmen. They all wore dark clothing without markings and they resembled the killers I had seen two days earlier in the restaurant.

A strong hand grabbed me firmly and pushed me back against the wall. I was exhausted but panic raced through my body. I was spreadeagled by one of the men, and frisked.

'You are friendly, aren't you?' I spluttered, extending my hand for him to shake.

Nothing was said and he didn't take my hand. He looked at me cautiously – and he began to grin. I could see his deep brown eyes, and his white teeth, but the rest of his face was black with smoke marks. I sensed his calmness and composure and found this reassuring. He gestured to me to stand against the wall. I complied but very gingerly stretched my aching arm out again to shake his hand. I didn't want to make any sudden movement, in case they thought I might be armed, but it was important for me to express my thanks in the only way I thought appropriate.

I was led out of the room, with one of the others in front and two behind me.

Everything suggested that I was being rescued. Yet I still wasn't sure. But this turned out to be the Black Cat Commandos – the elite National Security Guards – and I was being taken to safety along with other survivors. The Black Cats were formed in 1985 as a unit inspired by the UK's SAS – ironically, in the very same year that my brother had perished at sea, the unit that was to save my life was being inaugurated. They have become an important element in safeguarding the unity of India.

They were wearing bullet-proof vests than can withstand an AK-47 bullet at point-blank range. I learned that their weapons were Heckler & Koch sub-machine guns. This was the sound that I had heard so often in the past few hours.

But I wasn't out of the woods yet. Not by a long chalk.

I walked out of Room 1478 on my own. I emerged into

a scene of devastation and grime. I looked over the balcony, which had been shot to bits. It was a grotesque scene. Bodies were slumped on the ground far below. Barefoot, and wearing my smoke-impregnated jeans and a filthy shirt, I picked my way through the broken glass and debris that littered the sodden carpet. I was escorted to a room on the corner of the 14th floor. I was focusing on the fact I was alive, but I still didn't know if these were my real saviours, or a group of terrorists rounding us up as bargaining-chip hostages to secure their own release.

I was taken into a bedroom identical to mine, where there were about six other bedraggled looking people: two men and a woman from Spain, an Australian and a smart young Indian businessman. It was relief to be with others.

'Are these guys friendly forces?' I asked.

'We're not sure,' said a tall, fresh-faced guy with an Australian accent. 'They haven't said anything to us. Just told us to wait in here.'

There was still gunfire going on in the hotel. I could see that the others were extremely shaken. But the young Indian tried to reassure us.

'These are the Black Cats. You're going to be safe.'

The Australian introduced himself as Phil Sweeney. He was able to relay to his colleagues in the Australian High Commission that I was safe, and they passed this news onto British Embassy staff. Phil worked for the Australian Wings Academy at the Gold Coast Airport in Coolangatta, and, as we waited in the 14th floor corridor for the all-clear, we talked about our experiences, which were remarkably similar.

We stayed in this room for a further, agonising, 30 minutes. We were all hyper, chatting excitedly, relieved to share our war stories with fellow survivors. I didn't feel any sense of euphoria at this stage. Yes, there was a sense of relief, but I still wasn't sure what was going on. I didn't want to believe it quite yet. After all, I was still in this shattered hotel.

One of the Spaniards was Alvaro Abbad, who was the Director-General of Isolux Corsan, an engineering and construction business in Madrid. He was middle-aged, a suave, charismatic individual, although he looked decidedly dishevelled. He took out a crumpled packet of Fortuna cigarettes and offered me one. I took it from him and held it between two fingers while Alvaro clicked open his lighter.

'What am I doing? I don't smoke,' I said.

'It's OK, it won't kill you,' he laughed. I politely declined and pushed it back into the packet.

It was after 3.30pm local time when the Black Cats returned and gestured to us to follow. We were led along the corridor and told to crouch down behind the lifts shafts. Perhaps it wasn't the best thing to do, but I decided that now I would risk phoning Irene. I had such pent-up emotion, I just wanted to hear her voice. I pressed her name on the mobile phone and listened while it connected and began to ring. I didn't know what to say.

Back in Macduff it was 10am. The irrepressible Hunt clan had returned to continue the vigil and the living room had filled once again. Irene's peace and quiet had been short-lived. She had received a call at 3am, after dropping off to sleep for 20 minutes. It was Lynne: she reported they had received an email from me after a long lull. There had been grave concerns in Gogarburn but the email was a glimmer of good news. Then at 5.45am Carole and Clifford reappeared, urging Irene to go back to bed. Instead, she took a shower and another day began in earnest. By mid-morning, the television was blaring away. Irene heard the phone ring and shouted to Carole to answer it. She picked it up, expecting an update from Lynne, but exclaimed: '*Roger!*'

Irene shivered. She dashed to the phone, took the handset from Carole and moved out into the hall to hear more clearly away from the increasing hub-bub of excitement.

'Hello.'

'Are you out?' she said.

'No.'

Irene struggled to hear what was being said. My monosyllabic answer gave her a sense that something wasn't right and she began to panic. She could tell I was still in the Oberoi, and she shouted for Karine to get Lynne on the other phone line.

Hearing her voice and being able to say I was alive was overwhelming. But I knew the ordeal wasn't over yet. Irene thought that I had been caught by terrorists and that somehow I had been able to snatch a secret call home. She asked me another question.

'Are you with safe people?'

'I don't know.'

'Can you tell me where you are?'

'In a room.'

'Who are you with?'

'About six other people.'

During this tense exchange, Lynne had answered her phone and Irene was writing down the conversation, which was then being relayed by Karine to Lynne.

'Are you safe?'

'No.'

'Are you with safe people?'

'I'm not sure.'

Just then there was another ear-shattering blast. The reverberations from a stun grenade blew the phone out of my hand and knocked me over. It's a memory that my wife and I will take to our graves. The phone was thrown out of my hand and it broke into bits on the floor. My new acquaintances dived further for cover on the floor behind the lift shafts.

Irene had heard my voice – and then had it taken away from her seconds later. There had been a resounding cheer in Macduff. Now there was distress and pandemonium. Lynne was still on the phone with Karine, and Irene grabbed hold of it to recount what had just happened. To hear me briefly, to hear the strain in my voice, then to hear a noise which she described later as being like a film she had once seen when an oil tanker exploded in a tunnel with the flames whooshing out. The phone had gone dead. Irene became convinced that I was a hostage and that these were my last words. She had no idea whether I had been injured or killed in the blast. Throughout the whole ordeal, this was by far her greatest moment of agony.

'*He's not coming home,*' she cried to Lynne.

And for the only time throughout the whole ordeal, she lost her temper – shouting with fear and frustration. She wanted to know what was happening to me; thinking that my bank colleagues knew much more and were not telling her. She truly believed I was dead.

On the landing in the Oberoi we were all dazed, still sprawled on the floor. Then a figure in dark military uniform carrying a pistol emerged, and revealed himself as an Indian Army officer.

'We're still clearing the rooms of gunmen. We're making sure because some of the dead bodies might be booby-trapped. There will be another two blasts – and then we'll be free to move you down and out of the hotel. Sorry for the delay.'

'Can I go back and collect my bag and belongings in Room 1478?' I asked.

He consulted with another soldier who had arrived and was now speaking into a crackling walkie-talkie.

'OK, but be quick,' he nodded.

I gingerly picked my way back along the corridor, eyeing every doorway for any lone snipers. I heard more explosions as rooms were being blown out with Black Cat grenades. It was absolutely freaky, returning to this five-star hellhole. I opened the cupboard, grabbed my travellers' suitcase and cranked it open. I pulled my smoke-blackened shirts off the rails, and my work suits, forced them into my bag and shoved any other loose belongings I could see into my pocket. I couldn't wait to get out of this place.

It was strange surveying this room one last time: beforehand it had always seemed so luxurious and spacious, especially compared to the dozens of hotel rooms that I had stayed in over the years. Now it looked so tiny after being transformed into my haven of survival. In my haste, I overlooked my camera which actually contained many positive images of my Mumbai visit.

From: Chanel Rock
Sent: Friday 28 November 10:28
To: Roger Hunt
Subject: VERY URGENT: From Andrew

Rog I understand that the line is interrupted when you spoke with Irene. I know you now have Indian Military with you and the British Met Police are working with them to help you. I want to confirm to you that the guys with you now are on our side; they will help you. Please stay calm and stay safe Rog, we are very nearly there now mate. I am still here for you.

Andrew

Then there was another blast as I left the room and rejoined the cowering group at the lift shaft. I replied to Andrew:

> Thanks. Still on my original floor with guards. Explosions taking place.

I urgently needed to contact Irene again. At 10.10am, ten minutes after my phone was blown out of my hand, I tried again, using another hostage's phone. I struggled with the number but I was able to get through again. I had no appreciation of how stupefied and confused I had become.

'It's me. They are blasting the rooms and I lost my phone out of my hand,' I said when I got through.

'Are you OK, are you safe?' she asked.

'I'm not sure.'

'But are you in a safe place with friendly forces?'

'I think so, but I don't feel safe.'

'Can you speak?'

'Briefly, they still have a couple of rooms to clear before they can think about taking us out. Irene, I will need to go. They are away to blast another room.'

'Bye, love you.'

Irene was getting very limited responses. It still wasn't making a lot of sense to her. This compounded her fears. In my defence, I was exhausted, dehydrated and disorientated. Still traumatised, I couldn't quite believe I had survived.

It took some time before I started to regain a semblance of composure. I was having to readjust to what I was seeing with my own eyes. It was only now, after all those lonely hours in my room, that I was able to start piecing together the snippets of what had been going on around me. I was told that a terrorist group based in Pakistan called Lashkar-e-Taiba was believed to be responsible for the attack. I'm afraid it meant nothing to me at the time. The gunmen I had seen were part of a group who had attacked a number of places across Mumbai.

'What are they fighting for?' I asked.

'These terrorists see India as part of a Western alliance against Islam. It's their Holy War. A group calling themselves the Deccan Mujahideen have claimed responsibility. Their aim has been to kill Brits and Americans in Mumbai.'

So I was one of their prime targets. But it was also explained that the attack on Indian soil and in Mumbai was likely to provoke antagonism and tension between India's Hindu and Muslim communities. I had only seen three gunmen, but I was under the impression many more were involved. I was amazed when I heard that there were only ten people; surely they had others who were helping?

We made the journey down the fire escape stairs from the 14th floor. Before entering a back door into the stairwell, I snatched another look over the balcony. Down below, Indian nationals had been given the all-clear signal to enter the hotel and there was a hive of activity as they began the grim process of identifying and recovering the bodies from the Tiffin. On every flight of steps we stopped to look around, carefully stepping over the debris. As we filed down further to the lower levels there was intense smoke damage, blood on the walls and bullet holes everywhere. On the floor, there were jagged shards of glass, powdered masonry and spent cartridges. There were also discarded flip-flops and sandals – I wondered who they belonged to and where the owners of this footwear now were.

CHAPTER TWENTY

The Acrid Taste of Freedom

MY EYES WERE temporarily blinded by the intense Mumbai daylight as I emerged from the Oberoi 42 hours after the horrific events began. At the front door, a lectern was set up and an Indian official asked me my name and my room number. A porter stepped forward to help me with my suitcase. I was greeted by Tim Wilsey, an adviser to RBS, who had also been caught up in the attacks. He was delighted to meet me and I know the feeling was mutual.

Still barefoot, I was guided out into the hotel car park by the authorities and finally led to safety. Tim directed me around the corner from the hotel into the street adjacent to the ABN Amro building where I had been working a few days earlier. Normally this street was teeming with people, traffic and noisy activity, but now it was silent with not a soul in sight. I felt my Blackberry vibrate in my pocket – and I took a call from Dave Astill, the Metropolitan Police officer who had tried to speak to me before.

'It's Dave here. Where are you?'

'I'm out of the hotel, I'm in the street,' I replied.

'Who are you with?'

'A group of Indians have taken my things and are leading us up a quiet street.'

'Roger, listen carefully. I need you to describe to me exactly what they are wearing!'

I felt a sudden surge of adrenalin. This was a strange question – it made me think that there were new concerns for me to consider, and that I was walking right back into further danger.

'I'm with Tim. Everything is OK.'

'That's great. Take care and see you soon,' he said and signed off.

We walked in silence down the empty street. Tim and I were both engrossed in our own worlds: we were survivors. We turned left at the end of the road, and a moustachioed policeman ushered us through a cordon into another road. Within an instant, we were greeted by a huge crowd. People were cheering from behind the barriers. Some were stretching out their hands to touch me, shake my hand or pat my back. It was like royalty on walkabout.

We were steered over into a makeshift tented building, which was being used as a debriefing centre by the International Red Cross. There was a neat row of fold-away tables, with various people sitting speaking to officials in uniform. While I was waiting at the Red Cross shelter I saw Phil, the Australian colleague of another trapped Aussie called Garrick Harvison, and I inquired how he was doing.

'Fine, mate. At least I'm getting out of here. We're the lucky ones. Hundreds have lost their lives in this.'

I sensed his distress. He told me all of his party of six were alive, except one.

'I was on the mobile to my mate and he just told me the room phone had rung. He'd bloody well answered and was told someone from reception would be up to see him. That was a terrorist on the line,' he said.

He had made the fatal mistake of answering the room phone – and lost his life. I swallowed hard as I remembered how close I had been to answering the two calls I'd received. My throat was sore.

Australian wine exporter Garrick Harvison, after 20 hours trapped in his room under gun fire, had actually been able to speak directly to the Australian Broadcasting Corporation. He reported he was lying on the floor in a ball, pillows around him, eating Toblerone bars, drinking Coke and keeping quiet. He had his door barricaded and could hear the gunshots. He said the room phone had rung. Luckily he didn't answer. The caller left a message saying they were hotel security, but Garrick reckoned, correctly, that this was a hoax.

Garrick had brilliant support from the Australian Government; he had spoken to the federal police, the New South Wales police, the Department of Food and Trade, and Austrade. He said this was a great help, despite the fact that there was so much misinformation going about. When he was freed he spoke again to a news reporter. He said he had been kept up to speed, with information fed to him regularly:

> Unfortunately for the last 12 to 16 hours the updates were: 'You'll be out soon, we're clearing the hotel.' So, you keep thinking an hour, an hour, an hour, and you just keep going. I guess in actual fact, if you want to analyse it, that's probably a good thing to do because we just lived one hour at a time, and that's probably what got us through.

I felt much the same as Garrick. He appears to have been better informed about the final rescue and at the end he knew that the right people – the Black Cats – were coming through his hotel door to get him. He'd been told by the Australian Federal Police what they would be wearing and how to identify them. I had none of this information, and in retrospect it might have helped me in those desperate moments when the door was kicked open.

The soles of my feet were filthy, my shoulder and right side were aching heavily. I was black and blue with bruises. I'd walked through broken glass and had a minor cut. Here I was able to explain who I was, and gave a brief summary of my ordeal. I reached in my wallet and exchanged my business card with the others who had been escorted out of the hotel with me. I also wanted to phone Irene. This time, I was more certain, speaking briefly but more reassuringly.

'It's still some way to go – but I think it's going to be all right.'

At last, Irene really began to think I might be heading home safely. She called Lynne again. Having recovered her cool, she apologised for her brief outburst and they arranged a conference call with Niall McGuinness, another RBS colleague, to discuss my return to Scotland.

Meanwhile, I was handed a half-litre bottle of water. Without hesitating, I ripped off the blue cap and tentatively sipped a few drops. I knew that the human body needs to take its time when rehydrating itself: those first mouthfuls were sore and I had to swallow hard as my throat felt swollen. I thought again about the Indian kids at the airport – this is what they must feel like every day.

I was approached by a man in a jacket and casual shirt, who announced he was from the British Embassy. He proffered his business card.

'Hi, you must be Roger Hunt?'

'Yes, I am,' I croaked, my throat still rasping with pain.

'My name is Rob. I'm the token Scotsman in the embassy. We're here to ensure that you're properly looked after. How are you feeling?'

'Sore,' I rasped. 'I've got a lot of smoke in my chest.'

'Shall we take you to the hospital to get you checked out?'

Although my side was sore and I had smoke inhalation in my lungs, I was recovering pretty quickly now that I was out of the room.

'I don't need a hospital. Just get me out of here, if that can be arranged.'

'It certainly can.'

I pulled my Blackberry out of my pocket to check my emails again. There was an email from Andrew Sharman: good news was moving fast.

From: Chanel Rock
To: Roger Hunt
Sent: Friday 28 November 11:41
Subject: UPDATE
Rog
I hear that you are now safe with our people and out of the hotel and have spoken with Irene. This is brilliant news mate, and I can't wait to see you soon for those beers. Safe trip home my friend.
Andrew

From: Roger Hunt
To: Chanel Rock
Sent: Friday 28 November 12:22
Subject: Re: UPDATE
Can you let the P and A TEAM know that I have got out of the hotel alive! Rog.

Rob and Tim steered me into a green Defender Land Rover, asked me to keep low, and we drove out from behind the hotel, through what appeared like a whole regiment of Indian soldiers, police and fire brigade. Tim explained he had been in the Leopold Café, a famous watering-hole for Western visitors, less than 30 minutes before it was attacked. Gunmen had sprayed the café with bullets, killing several people.

I knew I'd missed my scheduled Friday morning flight, and for a split second I thought about Bharat waiting for his tip – and probably cursing his bad luck. Then my Blackberry pinged again; I got a fright after having its tone switched off. It was Andrew Sharman emailing again to tell me that there had been cheering and team huddles in P&A and P&E.

I was taken by Land Rover, driven by the British consulate official, a short distance down the road. We pulled up for a few moments and I looked back at the other side of the Oberoi. This fabulous hotel was a smouldering shell: there were very few windows left intact and there were black smoke marks on scores of the windows.

Tim explained we were switching vehicles, just to get away from all the action. Tim did this to save me facing the massed ranks of the international media, who were waiting for eyewitness statements.

'There's nothing to worry about. You're in safe hands now,' he tried to assure me.

We switched and Tim said we were heading to Gavin's apartment at Wellington Mews, only a short distance away. The streets were so quiet it was like a ghost town as we drove away from this shocking scene.

Within a few minutes, we arrived at the high wrought-iron electronic gates of Gavin's luxury residence. There was a police car and several armed guards with rifles manning the gate. We showed our security passes, the police tapped our wing mirror and waved us into the front driveway of the towered modern complex.

Everything was still in a whirl for me, but the fresh air felt very good. We took the lift up to the 7th floor.

'You're safe here,' I was assured.

'I'm not so sure about that,' I answered, rather sceptically.

'I've seen the force of the terrorist operation, there's no way a few security guards armed with old rifles can hold back what I've seen.'

There was huge relief in seeing Gavin again. He hugged me tight and invited me into his spacious apartment. I was alive to tell my tale. Now I wanted to hear his side of the story. Later he told me I was so filthy, with my face covered in soot and my fingernails black as coal, that I wouldn't have been out of place as a beggar on the street.

'It's great to see you safe, Rog,' he said.

'It's just unbelievable to be out of that, Gavin. I can't really take it all in at the moment.'

'Would you like us to check you out at the hospital?'

'No thanks, I'm just a bit bruised and sore and probably need a drink.'

'Of course,' he replied. 'Would you like something to eat too?'

'No, I still feel pretty sick with the smoke.'

'Something light to nibble on then?'

'Cheers, but no thanks,' I replied.

'Then a beer it is,' he said.

He disappeared into his kitchen. I heard the fridge click open and a clink of glass before he brought back a chilled bottle of Beck's with the top removed. This was really the first proper drink I'd had in 40 hours. Its coolness soothed my throbbing throat although it hardly touched the sides. Gavin said that I could stay in his apartment that evening and get a flight back to London the following morning, after a good night's rest. Or else he might be able to get me on the later evening flight that night. I was in no doubt.

'If you can get me on the evening flight tonight, I'll definitely go on that one,' I said.

I was wretched, stinking and my feet were filthy. I had a

shower. It was such a wonderfully refreshing feeling standing under the spray – yet I found it hard to wash away all the grit and grime. I was still unnerved by the whooshing of the water and I listened intently to every strange sound of the pipes in the apartment.

Stepping out and drying myself, I felt a lot better. I stared in the mirror at my face with three days' growth on my chin. I'd also lost a stone in weight. I managed to find a clean suit in my case that wasn't covered in smoke. Meanwhile, Gavin had put my jeans and shirt into his washing machine and they were soon being tumble-dried.

I took a second beer from the fridge. The adrenalin was still coursing through my body and I just couldn't settle down. There wasn't a sense of elation about being freed. I actually felt guilt. I was alive when so many others, including local people and the policemen and security forces who put their lives on the line, were now dead. It was mid-afternoon but the curtains were already closed. I soon found out why. Gavin's Wellington Mews has a spectacular vista of the city. When I peeled back the drapes, I could see the Taj Mahal Palace & Tower Hotel a short distance away. It was still on fire. It was only then that I realised that this grand hotel had been hit as well.

The Taj was still burning on the left and on the right there was a thin pall of smoke at Nariman House, which was where I learned a Jewish Centre had been targeted. Here Rabbi Gavriel Noach Holtzberg and his family had been taken hostage, then murdered. Gavin witnessed Indian commandos being lowered onto the roof of the building by helicopter. The terrorists had perished in the assault.

'Is that the roof of the Taj?' I said, pointing outside.

'Yes, there's still an operation going on there.'

I had a flash of panic. We were still in the middle of a

triangle of death and destruction. This looked and felt like a war zone. Just how safe was I there in Gavin's home? If the terrorists in the Taj had been able to activate the rocket launchers they had hidden, then we would have been sitting targets in Wellington Mews.

'How can we be safe?' I said.

I don't think I heard an answer. The door buzzer sounded and moments later we were joined by Kate Averre and her husband Nick. We stood for a moment in silence looking at the Taj, then they started to fill me in. I began to understand that this was on a far bigger scale that I had ever imagined.

I recalled we had all been dining in the Taj's restaurant until 11pm on the Tuesday evening. Now we looked at each other, without saying it, but I think we all thought it: how fortunate we had been. That same restaurant was attacked the following evening, and we nearly booked for that time. We would most certainly have perished if we'd been there 24 hours later.

Tim and Gavin told me that two anti-terrorist officials were on their way up to see me. Dave Astill from the hostage negotiations team and Phil Williams from counter-terrorist command were going to take a statement. I did feel a bit nervous, but I thought it was the right thing to do. Kate and Nick offered to leave the room, but I was happy that they should stay and hear about my experiences.

They had been caught up in the attacks too; Gavin told me about how he, Kate, Nick and Mhairi, who had only just arrived on the Wednesday afternoon and checked into the Oberoi, had been stuck in the Maresh restaurant, and how scared they had been. They had to stay overnight with all the lights out. It was a terrifying ordeal for them too. We now all shared a common bond.

I took a small bite of banana. I gagged as it burned the

raw inside of my gullet.

I asked for another beer, but Gavin was concerned about me. He wanted me to eat something more. Instead, he arranged for some hot tea: a sensible decision.

Tim asked me if it was OK if the anti-terrorist squad recorded our conversation. I thought this was part of the drill. Dave Astill laid down a digital recorder on the table. It would be easier and more practical when compiling a report back in London, he explained. Initially, Tim refrained from committing us to this.

'If any small detail can avoid anyone having to go through this ordeal again, then I'm happy to make a statement.' I said.

Tim nodded approvingly and we began.

'Did you have any survival training?' he asked as a starter.

I shook my head – none at all.

I went on to explain my ordeal in some detail. I spent 45 minutes taking them through it, step-by-step. After I'd finished, Dave was pleased. He appreciated the clarity and thoroughness of the answers considering what I'd just come through. I was told that I should be proud of my decisions.

I was told my strategy had certainly contributed to saving my life: staying in the room when every instinct was to get out; wrapping the wet towel around my head to keep the smoke off my face; not using the minibar or answering the phone, which might have given away that I was in the room; covering the Blackberry and mobile phone with a hand towel; and not using the toilet. Of course I was extremely lucky, but those other things all added up.

'Roger, you're now part of an elite club: humans who have been through a near-death experience,' said Phil.

'It's a club I'd rather not have been a part of,' I said. 'But I guess you can't change history.'

With the debriefing session over, I was able to phone Irene

again. This time we were able to have a proper chat. And I also made a few more calls and thank-yous to my colleagues in Gogarburn.

In the weeks when RBS was going through turmoil in the banking collapse and its leadership was being pilloried, my survival was one piece of great news. The cheering went on for a while in one part of the RBS HQ. I could never thank my colleagues enough for all their endeavour on my behalf, but I knew that if the tables were turned we'd all have done the same for each other.

Gavin managed to get us all on the Friday evening flight. We gathered our bags and left his apartment and I sat in the car feeling dazed. As we approached the airport perimeter the traffic slowed to walking pace. I noticed there was a heavy police presence and armed guards checking every vehicle. I became nervous again, seeing the armed forces.

We pulled into the airport, jumped out of the car and pushed our baggage into the departure area, which was heaving with people, most standing in long lines with trolleys and bags waiting to reach the check-in counters. Two British Airways staff appeared and escorted us right to the front of the queue to check in.

'We're safe now,' said Gavin.

He made a gesture moving his eyes towards the khaki-clad Indian security forces inside the terminal. I wasn't sure I quite shared Gavin's optimism.

The firepower of the terrorists in the Oberoi had been withering. They had been able to pin down elite forces for hours. The airport guards with their ancient rifles without body armour just didn't look like a match for determined suicidal terrorists with sub-machines guns and grenades.

I kept that negative thought to myself.

CHAPTER TWENTY-ONE

Family Reunion

THE JOURNEY HOME was harder than I ever imagined. I knew I was going to see Irene and the kids, but I was permanently distracted by flashbacks. It was like a horror film replaying and rewinding on a loop in my head.

I thought of the Australian businessman who answered the room phone and was dead. I replayed in my head dozens of times the decision not to take a dessert from the sweet trolley or have a coffee. If I'd stayed in the restaurant another few minutes it would have cost me my life. I remembered the unbridled laughter of the birthday cake ceremony. Then I recalled the smoke and heat of the fire. How I was suffocating – but somehow managed to put the air conditioning off. There were numerous moments when I thought: 'This is the end.'

The overpowering memory was of the bodies of Alan Scherr and his daughter. I thought a great deal about Naomi in the months following the attack. Her roommate at the Oberoi, Helen Connolly, spoke movingly about her in an interview (she was the woman I'd seen with Naomi in the pool). On the Wednesday evening she had taken Naomi down to the Tiffin for some sushi, then they had joined their friends in the Kandahar. She recalled the attack: 'My impression was of a kid playing a video game trying to get a perfect score, because he just kept shooting and shooting. Naomi let out a scream, but no words. I prayed that she would be quiet, because I thought that as long as she made sounds of life, he would keep shooting her.'

Helen was grazed by a bullet. When she lifted one of Naomi's arms she realised it was lifeless.

I felt an acute sense of remorse that this gorgeous girl, who reminded me of my own children, was dead, while I was alive. That awful sense of guilt returned. There had been a death toll of nearly two hundred, of whom many were workers in the hotel. There were dozens of tragic stories. Yet I had survived.

I was reunited with my RBS colleagues in the executive departure lounge at the airport. They were sitting in cushioned seats around a table and they were so pleased to see me – it was mutual. I was thankful they hadn't been caught up in any of the killing. My RBS colleagues chatted animatedly for some time, but I didn't feel I was properly engaged.

Mhairi Thomson asked me how I was feeling and had I seen anything. For the second time, I started to tell my story and it dawned on her that I had witnessed some terrible scenes and was incredibly fortunate to be alive. She glanced at Gavin, who was sitting on my left, and grabbed my hand to comfort me. As she gripped my hand, her eyes began to fill with tears. She understood the intensity of what I had been through and my miraculous escape. Then it dawned on her that had she declined Gavin's invitation to have supper on the Wednesday evening, she too would have been stuck in the hotel. I looked her straight in the eye and reassured her that I was comfortable talking about everything, but she could see the hurt that was bottled up inside me, in particular the pain of seeing others slaughtered and being powerless to do anything about it. My voice started to break with emotion as I tried to explain seeing a young life ended in front of me. I was close to tears, so I excused myself and headed into the airport washroom. I pressed on the tap and splashed cool water over my face. I felt lousy. I had now gone 60 hours without sleep and my body was rebelling.

As I returned to Mhairi, Gavin and the others, I saw a group of passengers huddled around one of the flat-screen televisions in the departure lounge. A local news channel was on – reporting events with graphic detail. Gavin suggested that perhaps I should wait until I'd recovered sufficiently before watching the news, but I was drawn to it.

I was intensely tired, yet my mind was still racing – I was somehow still awake and it was after 2am. Gavin was called away and ended up in a discussion with an airline official. I knew the flight was very busy and might be full. I became concerned that we might not get on this flight; I shuddered at the thought of another night in Mumbai. Gavin was happier when he returned, to tell me that we were going home First Class, upgraded from Business Class.

I phoned home again and spoke to the kids for the first time. It was wonderful to hear their voices. The call was just long enough for me to tell them how much I loved them all. Moments later, Gavin and I were called for the flight. Twenty minutes later I was in my pod. The two air stewardess were very attentive and seemed aware that I had been caught up in the siege. It seemed like an age before the plane door was finally slammed shut, and locked.

Within minutes the jet was speeding along the runway and I became so exhilarated I wanted to punch the air. I decided this would be inappropriate – but I was ecstatic that we were heading home. I couldn't sleep and paced about the cabin for much of the flight; I was running on empty, the hours of high-octane adrenaline were draining away. I switched on the in-flight television screen and clicked to the news channel. Now I had time to properly digest the events in Mumbai and the tiny part I had played in the whole drama. I watched the footage of the burning Taj Mahal hotel, then I saw the attack on the train station, and for the first time I observed how close I had been to this when Bharat the driver had tried to insist we go and see it; I saw the images of the bullet-raked Leopold Café; I was shocked as details were recounted of the attacks on hospitals and the Jewish Centre.

This was still a live situation. While I was on the flight home, there were still people trapped in the Taj. I could imagine their state of mind only too well. I realised that this whole event would not be over until every last hostage was free to go home to their families.

Tim told me later that the bank had booked him into the Trident Hotel in March 2009. He bumped into the sales manager he had befriended on the Wednesday evening and they had had a long talk. The guy explained to Tim that the terrorists had planted two bombs, each containing 9kg of RDX, outside the Trident and the Oberoi. These were the deafening blasts that had caused the fires. The explosion broke the windows up to the 16th floor on the other side of the hotel. He said the terrorists had killed six in the Trident before crossing over to the Oberoi, where 26 people were killed. I was surprised when he told me that only four were hotel guests.

It emerged that the young terrorists at the Oberoi had not known how to switch on the bathroom taps to get a drink of water: this suggested they were poor recruits from rural tribal areas of Pakistan, where they had been radicalised into joining this death mission. After the killings, the terrorists had hidden in rooms on the 15th floor, directly above Room 1478. That's why I heard so much gunfire. The explosions were the Black Cats blowing open the doors to find them hunkered down. It took two days to find them. Then when they stumbled on the room where the terrorists were ready for their last stand, there was the major gun battle that I heard. This was right above me. In the later stages, most of the noises on my corridor and past my door were the special forces... but I didn't know this.

As the jet continued towards Britain, my body was pleading with me to rest. Some people say that counting sheep helps you fall asleep, I was calculating that I had been awake for about 66 hours when I dropped off for the first time. I had been too frightened to sleep before, knowing that I am susceptible to snoring. I managed about two hours of uninterrupted slumber, before a jolt of turbulence woke me and brought me bolt upright. I looked around in the cabin and everyone else had their heads down. The senior air steward approached and kindly offered to make me something to eat and a drink. He could see my restlessness. Unobtrusively, while the others slept, he asked me if I'd like to talk about what happened. He didn't want to pry — only if it helped, he said. I was grateful for his interest and over the next half hour I recounted my tale. It really allowed me to unload some deeper thoughts, and I was able to return for another hour or so of more restful sleep.

When we landed at Heathrow, the captain read out a list of people who were to contact the Metropolitan Police when they left the plane. As Gavin and I stood with our bags preparing for the pressurised cabin door to open, I listened to the roll call, hearing Mark Abell's name among the list, before the last name: '... and Mr Roger Hunt'. Then an elderly lady passenger who had been sitting behind me touched my shoulder. 'That's you isn't it?' she said with a friendly smile. It was weird because I don't know how she knew.

Those on the list were met by armed British police and some representatives of the security services. We were led out a side door and into Land Rovers and driven to a quieter area of the terminal building. It was there I waited for my flight to see Irene. Gavin was still by my side and we sat together on the hour-long Heathrow to Aberdeen flight, which was full. We didn't say much, but our shared experiences over the past few days had brought us very close. I was grateful for his friendship and for everything he had done for me. I'd taken this flight dozens of times over the years, but this time it was a clear, bright day and I stared out the window, engrossed in the patchwork of greens, golds and browns below. I was so glad to be back in Britain, and heading north.

I arrived back in Aberdeen at 10.30am on Saturday morning. Again there was an announcement in the cabin over the tannoy: 'Would the passengers returning from Mumbai please make themselves known to the officials when they depart this aircraft.' I heard a few guffaws from some burly oil workers who joked that there wouldn't be anyone from India on this flight. In fairness, they were far removed from this episode on the other side of the world; but I was still reliving every moment and emotion.

Gavin offered to come with me all the way back to Macduff, but I thought it better for him to return to his home in London, where he hadn't been for several months.

When we landed in Aberdeen Gavin patted my shoulder as we stood in the aircraft aisle awaiting our turn to leave.

'Roger, you need to remember. This is going to be very difficult.'

'I know,' I replied grimly.

'Just prepare yourself – because things will never, ever be the same again.'

I knew what he meant. Somehow I had survived – and my

life would be changed by the experience.

Irene and Lisa were on their way to the airport, driven by Ian Elliott, RBS's media advisor. He had made all the arrangements from the Scottish end. The day before, he had to find my car in the airport car park – and Jocky, Karine's husband, had been kind enough to drive it home with a spare set of keys. When Irene and Lisa reached Dyce they were given a police escort right through to the back of the airport where the VIPs or Royals land before heading off to Balmoral or on official duties. Irene told me later that she felt everyone was helpful and genuinely cared for my safe return.

I was escorted into a smaller terminal building and I could see Irene and Lisa standing together through the glass partition. Then they clocked me, despite my four-day beard with its flecks of gray. They could see me and wanted to run to me. Their faces lit up as I approached them. We didn't say a word. I threw my arms around them both; we all just hugged each other as tightly as we could. It was the best feeling in the world, a moment in my life which I will freeze-frame for ever. I breathed in Irene's gentle perfume, savouring every touch from her. I felt elated and so lucky to be nearly home. There were tears in all of our eyes and I had a lump in my throat. Irene and Lisa were sobbing and smiling at the same time. I also couldn't wait to see Stephanie and Christopher. They had decided to stay at home because they knew how emotional this would have been all together.

The local Grampian Police CID wanted to debrief me before I was fully united with my family, so I was taken into a windowless room, where Irene, Lisa and Ian had to wait another 90 agonising minutes before I returned. Ian drove us home with a police escort out of the airport. I could hardly speak and I sat gripping Irene's hand tightly. I spent most of the journey staring out of the window at the Aberdeenshire countryside. All the events of the last few days were replaying again and again in my head. I had felt certain that I was going to die and I would have given anything just to see my family again. Now Irene was sitting next to me. Each time I looked at her or Lisa, or listened to their voices, I was overwhelmed. I had to fight back tears as I realised how near I had been to losing them. I also began thinking about what I really wanted from my life now and what I needed to change. I kept saying to myself: *I'm alive. I'm alive. I'm alive.*

We made it back to Macduff by 2pm on Saturday. There were special hugs and fresh tears from me for both Stephanie and Christopher. It was so wonderful to see them and touch them both. It was also so good to see family and friends who have been part of the incredible vigil for my return. I couldn't say much to people: I just hugged them all. The local press knew I was back and were now camped outside our house waiting for an interview. But I was too exhausted and I felt like a goldfish in a bowl. I simply wanted peace on our own. We all had unanswered questions, but in the meantime we simply wanted calm to return to our family. Everyone tried so hard to do the ordinary and familiar things for me – and we had the best fish and chips that evening for supper. But I knew that my life had changed for ever.

CHAPTER TWENTY-TWO

Aftermath

THE MEDIA DUBBED the Mumbai attacks as 'India's 9/11' and it became a massive international story, of which mine was simply one tiny fragment. As the dust began to settle and the investigations to find the culprits and ringleaders went on in India and Pakistan, what had we all been able to learn?

On a personal level, I was learning how to readjust to normal life. I had recurring nightmares of mutilated bodies and death. Irene would gently shake me awake out of these awful dreams. Somehow one night I ended curled up on the floor in a dark corner of our bedroom. Shivering. What was going on? There were still too many unresolved matters playing around in my head; and that sense of guilt about having survived when so many others had perished.

After the first weekend the house began to see a stream of family, friends and wellwishers. My sister, Lynne, flew in from Abu Dhabi to settle in her own mind that I was all right. Lynne Highway made the four-hour journey from Edinburgh for the same reasons, although she had been in regular contact since my release. It was fantastic to see her – and thank her for her help. While she had been at the heart of the RBS's Incident Team, she was shocked to learn first-hand the graphic details of my time in the Oberoi.

The bank flew a trauma counsellor up from Bristol. She

was very kind and attentive, but after a single joint session Irene and I decided that we wanted to work this out for ourselves. There was no right or wrong way to deal with our trauma. The counsellor expressed her ease at our decision and felt we were certainly strong enough together to see through some of the challenges ahead.

During the day I hardly ventured out and the family collaborated in what they called 'Roger Sitting' – so I was seldom on my own for too long. Yet night after night, I would awaken bolt upright, and then walk through the house in the darkness, twitching back the curtains and looking out of the windows at the empty street. Irene would come and sit with me, and we'd often talk until sunrise.

Throughout the week the weather was mild and sunny yet all the blinds and curtains were closed to keep out the prying eyes of the press and media. Irene and the children followed my every move and announced in advance any noise they would make. They scanned the TV to censor programmes that they felt would be unsuitable and raced to catch every phone call before I did. In trying so hard to protect me they were over-compensating and I had virtually become a prisoner in my own home. Every visitor was vetted. I made a conscious decision to break this cycle and start putting some normality back into our lives.

Towards the end of the week I ventured out for the first time, past my favourite bakery, Duguids, where they still bake the world's best rowies (flat Aberdeen savoury rolls), and down into chilly Macduff. Everywhere people expressed their happiness at my safe return. The cold air braced me as I strode around these familiar streets, looking at them now in a very different light.

As the weeks and months went on after my return, I continued to follow the story. I was still keen to know who was behind the attacks – and what was their reason for it. This became part of my own healing. The sole surviving gunman, 21-year-old Mohammad Ajmal Kasab, initially pleaded guilty to taking part in the slaughter and waging war against India. He was the dark-haired, baby-faced gunman who was photographed in the railway station wearing a dark Versace designer label T-shirt, light grey trousers with pockets on the leg and carrying a backpack. He became the iconic image of the attacks. *The Scotsman* newspaper's front page on Friday morning carried a colour picture of a young man who looked like Ajmal Kasab. The headline read: 'He Looked Like Any Student... Seconds Later He Became the Young Face of Terrorism'. *The Times*, which was still calling the city by its old name, Bombay, also had the terrorist's image on the front page with a story which highlighted the political significance of the attacks:

> India pointed an accusing finger at Pakistan yesterday as commandos fought suspected Islamist terrorists through the corridors of two of Bombay's top hotels. Dozens of foreigners were still being held hostage or trapped in the buildings.

Ajmal Kasab said he came from Pakistan's Punjab region and was given a year's jihad commando training. He said he was following orders by phone. The Indian court charges accuse him of killing about 50 people. Then he later retracted his statement, saying he was tortured to make an admission, and that he had arrived in Mumbai to work in the Bollywood film industry. What was the truth? What was true was that nine other terrorists died in the ensuing gun battles.

And what of the leaders who ordered the killings? The Indian government charged 37 other people, who were all believed to be connected to the attacks, and thought to be in Pakistan. I wanted to know who those angry individuals at the other end of the mobile phone calls were, urging the young assailants to continue their killing. I understood that Hafiz Mohammed Saeed, the founder of Lashkar-e-Taiba, had been put under arrest in Pakistan, but he denied any involvement. Then there was Zaki-Ur-Rehman Lakhvi, who has been accused of being the mastermind, and Zarar Shah who confessed to being in constant contact with the gunmen during the siege.

Was Mumbai properly prepared for an attack like this? The city's Police Commissioner D. Sivanandan later admitted lapses and confusion in the early responses to this unprecedented assault on the city. How can ten men, albeit well-armed and equipped, hold up a city? I always felt that there were many more involved, and that ten people could not have sustained such firepower without help – or else stockpiles of ammunition and weapons.

I have not a single bad feeling about the Indian people and their fabulous country. While I'd still be nervous about returning, until my own demons are fully exorcised, there is no doubt that Indians, and Mumbai in particular, truly suffered because of the attacks. One of the saddest sights for me was the front page newspaper picture of the empty railway station with blood spattered across the concrete floor; the abandoned bags, rucksacks and plastic carrier bags; the bottles of water, and all of the dozens and dozens of flip-flops left by the dead and those who had stampeded for cover. It reminded me of the similar scene I had witnessed in the aftermath of the Oberoi siege. The horror impinged on Indian nationals as well as on the Westerners the terrorists targeted. My fellow hostage, Mark Abell summed it up when he talked about the staff and police officers at the Oberoi: 'They took my luggage, put me in the lift, took me down to the lobby and walked me through the carnage. These people here have been fantastic, the Indian authorities, the hotel staff. They are a great advertisement for their land.'

My life converged with the ordinary people of Mumbai on that day; but I was privileged enough to have a large organisation looking after my welfare as best it could, and fortunate enough to return to a community that has its own particular problems but is, by-and-large, still law-abiding and relatively safe. If the terrorists achieved anything, they have awoken a resolve in moderate-minded people not to give in to bullies and murderers who seek change through the gun and the indiscriminate bomb.

Weeks later, I linked up with Gavin Reid and we talked about the events. He had the privilege of working with many Indian nationals during his months on the RBS project. He admired their resilience and courage in returning to normal as quickly as possible. He reminded me that there had been many other bombings in India – including a horrific train bombing where 187 people were killed – which hardly made more than a few lines in the British media. He said India had been targeted much more than Britain or America, and was often on the frontline in the so-called War on Terror, yet he was amazed how quickly people brushed themselves down and got on with life. They were optimistic in outlook, they wanted to better their family circumstances, and they were able to appreciate many of the basic virtues of life.

Some of this has become lost to us in the West, in a society hung up on banal celebrity and grab-what-you-can consumerism. I've come to revise my view of films, dramas and TV murder mysteries which show the relentless killing of people with guns, knives and bombs. Can it be right to package brutal slaughter as entertainment? And I'm shocked by the potentially desensitising effects of 'shoot-em-up' computer games. Seeing a real human being murdered in cold-blood is one of the most chilling things that one can ever experience. It has left me with an acute awareness that all life is precious and how dangerous it is to present violence as a prime-time pastime.

My colleagues in the bank were fantastic. There was an outpouring of wonderful emails from people all over RBS. They had been advised not to contact me while I was stuck in the room, but now they were free to send their thoughts, kind wishes and jokey welcome backs. It was incredibly moving. There were scores of cards – one from Richard Fulham typifies the sentiment which aided my recuperation. His card read: 'Friends are the sunshine of life' and inside was a handwritten note: 'Your courage, stoicism and grit are an example to us all. Sitting at the other end in Gogarburn was bad enough, but your tenacity was incredible. I'm proud to have you as a friend and colleague. Prouder still to have you back home.'

One of the funniest came from Vic Bicocchi, the bank's head of corporate development, who said my whole experience reminded him of a friend called Jim Murphy who was stuck overnight in the Dufftown Branch on the 2nd January many years ago with no toilet roll or coffee. 'You certainly have one up on him now!' said Vic. I got the joke.

Our family and friends in Macduff couldn't understand why we didn't want to throw a big party – something we might have done in normal circumstances. But I was still recovering and I knew in my heart that others elsewhere were coming to terms with their loss and grief in India – I didn't want to celebrate, so our festive period was subdued in 2008. Just before Christmas, Irene and I thought it would be appropriate to place a public notice in the local paper, the *Banffshire Journal*:

HUNT

Roger, Irene, Lisa, Christopher and Stephanie would like to thank all the family and friends, staff at MPS [Macduff Primary School] and the RBS team for the many telephone calls, flowers and cards received with messages of support and hope. A special thanks to 'The House Crew' – you know who you are – for the round the clock support you gave Irene and the kids. Lastly, and most importantly, to everyone in the Special Forces and behind the scenes for bringing Roger back home safely. Thank you all. As we will not be sending Christmas cards this year, we will take the opportunity to wish everyone a Merry Christmas and a Happy and Peaceful 2009.

I returned to work after two weeks, keen to restore 'normality' to my life. Lynne Highway arranged an audio call with Neil Roden, RBS's group HR director. He told me kindly to take all the time I needed to recover, and perhaps wait until the New Year, but I said that I planned to be back at work the following Monday. And I was.

But after only a few months I decided to leave RBS. The ABN Amro merger was not a wise decision for Sir Fred and the bank, and the global banking crunch had a deep impact. Instead of expansion, there was now severe contraction and it required billions of pounds of UK government help to keep the bank going. While there remained a very professional staff committed to their work, the culture and aspiration weren't quite the same. The good days were over, perhaps not for good, but for some time to come. I have nothing but admiration for all the people I worked with in RBS. It is a fantastic organisation, whatever anyone says about it. But after 26 years what should have been a difficult decision, in the aftermath of the Oberoi, was very easy. I wanted to refocus my career with a much greater balance of time for those who mattered most in my life.

My experience in India was all very humbling and has had a profound impact on my own life. I now understand that there are so many parallel lives beyond my existence in Scotland. And there are times and places when human hatred collides with apathy, ignorance and the cushion of privilege. I will never take anything for granted again.

It is ironic, after years working in Peterhead, that I should return there to work. I'm now a senior manager within HM Prison at Peterhead, an imposing grey-granite penal establishment facing out onto the cold North Sea that 20 years earlier we would have taken a trip around in the car on a Sunday when there was little else to do. It is an interesting job in a completely new environment.

One of my RBS colleagues, Vesna Buric, asked me later if I believed in fate. I paused to consider this.

'I never have. However, my outlook is now different. I believe that fate does not determine your future, it simply allows you to have choices, some of which are determined by your own actions,' was how I replied.

On deep reflection, there were conscious and unconscious factors that contributed to my survival. Some might even call it yin and yang, as in the opposing principles of Chinese philosophy.

The unconscious path might have been when I decided to stay and work in Edinburgh instead of quitting the job after one week; my trip to Mumbai being brought forward by one week because of a local festival; the decision to switch to the Oberoi, rather than stay nearer to Mafatlal Mills; dining at the Taj Mahal on the Tuesday evening rather than the next night. Then on the fateful day, declining the opportunity to visit the train station, scene of so much bloodshed, despite Bharat's insistence; my delayed return to the Oberoi, which meant that I went into the Tiffin before my evening walk; eating the birthday cake at the office celebration and later refusing a sweet and a coffee, moments before the killers appeared.

And on the conscious side there were definite actions that allowed me to live: calculated decisions that I took. These were: to stay and ride out the fire and the smoke; to wet the towel with my urine; to switch off the air conditioning; to set up the room to look as if it was unoccupied. My choice not to trigger the minibar at reception was also a vital part of my strategy, and I stuck to it despite my terrible thirst. Staying put, hunkered down, when there was an overwhelming desire to leave that room, saved my life. Other guests who tried to escape were mown down in cold blood. Not answering the phone calls to my room, and my pact of remaining silent, with no lights and no noise, were all conscious actions. It was a matter of be silent or be killed.

But I recalled what Phil Williams, of the Metropolitan Police's Counter Terrorism Command, had said to me in Gavin's flat an hour after my release. I'd been in a life and death situation where every decision I made enhanced or diminished my changes of survival. I felt a glow: I HAD BEATEN THEM. I HAD WON MY PERSONAL BATTLE.

Just before Christmas 2008, I received an email from Devendra Bharma, the vice president of the Oberoi Trident Hotel group. He paid tribute to the heroism of the law enforcement agencies and his hotel colleagues during the tragic events.

'We must not allow such acts of terrorism to disrupt our normal daily lives. I am sure you agree that all of us must come together and face this challenge with fortitude.'

He said the team had been working around the clock to re-open the Trident on 21 December, although the Oberoi would be closed for many more months. I applauded such an achievement and wondered at how they managed to repair the Trident so quickly.

He closed with the words, 'My team and I look forward to welcoming you at Trident, Nariman Point, Mumbai.' He wrote me a more personal letter on 15 December, saying:

> The last few days have been traumatic for all of us. We must defeat terrorism by resuming our normal daily lives. We know that you endured trying circumstances and anxiety during this period and we sincerely apologise. It was unfortunate that the circumstances were beyond our control. It is gratifying to all of us that you were evacuated safely from the hotel. While we lost some guests and ten colleagues, the National Security Guards and our staff members evacuated 450 guests and 700 staff members. We feel blessed. Let us pray for those who we could not save.

A few days later I received a follow-up phone call offering me a return visit with the salesman saying that everything was fine in the hotel, and somehow downplaying the whole episode. I understood completely what Mr Bharma and his team were trying to do: this was part of the Indian spirit we so admired. I thanked them profusely for the call, but I don't think I want to repeat the experience of staying in Room 1478. Not in this lifetime.

Each evening we count our blessings and celebrate our great fortune, looking forward to enjoying our children becoming adults and finding their own places in life. And yes, Andrew Sharman did buy me those beers in the Bistro.

VERDICT

IN MAY 2010, as the first edition of this book was going to print in Scotland, the story was still major television news in Mumbai. I guess it has a long way to run as the grieving goes on for hundreds of sorrowful people. At the end of April 2010, the Oberoi Hotel was finally reopened with three stunning new restaurants sweeping away the traces of the killings, although rooms start at an eye-watering £460 a night.

But, more significantly, on Thursday 6 May 2010, a court in India handed a death sentence to Mohammed Ajmal Kasab, the only surviving Pakistani gunman.

Judge ML Tahaliyani's sentence came three days after Kasab was found guilty of murder and waging war against India, and for his role in the attacks that claimed 166 lives. Kasab's lawyers launched an appeal, but on 21 February 2011 the Indian High Court upheld the death sentence. However Kasab could still appeal to the supreme court for clemency.

India blames the militant group, Lashkar-e-Taiba, for masterminding the attack, while the judge rejected arguments by Kasab's attorney, KP Pawar, that he had committed the crime under duress and pressure from Lashkar. The judge said Kasab joined the militant group on his own and trained to be a fighter.

'Such a person can't be given an opportunity to reform himself,' said the judge.

Death sentences in India are carried out by hanging.

Looking back, I can't help but wonder about this young man. The special prosecutor Ujjwal Nikam, said in an interview that he expected it would take at least a year for Kasab to be executed. So this sad story will go on for some time. Though India voted against a moratorium on capital punishment at the United Nations in 2007 and 2008, in practice the country has been veering away from applying the death penalty.

Speaking in a television interview, Ujjwal Nikam said Kasab was a complex person and very shrewd, but showed no remorse or repentance.

An earlier filmed confession to Indian police gave some indication of what kind of person he was. Kasab was shown lying on a hospital bed with his eyes closed. His top half naked and a rough blanket covering him. He has a dressing on a wound to his neck.

'Who persuaded you to go there?' he was asked by a middle-aged police officer with two silver stars on his epaulets.

'My father told me. "We are very poor. You will also earn money like others",' he said.

'Your own father?' asked the officer.

'Yes,' said Kasab. 'He said, "You will earn money like the others. It is not difficult. Your siblings will also get married. You will stay happy like others."'

He talked in Urdu about his mother, Noor Ilahee, who is a housewife and around 40 years old, and his father, Aamir, who works as a hawker in Lahore and is nearly 45 years old. He has three brothers and two sisters. He left school in 2000 and became a labourer, moving to Lahore, until 2005. He said he wasn't paid well for his work. Then his father introduced him to a man called Chacha from LeT, although his father was not a member. Chacha was a bearded man, around 45 years old, who would give his father money for his actions. He said Chacha had fought the Russians in Afghanistan. Kasab was then sent for training with 25 other boys. He was in Mansera when Benazir Bhutto, the former Pakistani premier, was assassinated after a political rally in December 2007.

Kasab said he was told it was a Jihad. He said: 'It's a very honourable and daring job. You earn respect, it's a work of God. You will earn lots of money and your poverty will be eliminated.'

The police chief asked him:

'What is the meaning of Jihadi?'

'I don't know. They didn't tell us. They told us this is a way to heaven,' he replied.

Whatever the truth, this was a father's son. As a father, the same age as Kasab's and with my son Christopher of a similar age to Kasab, I could not help but reflect on all of these terribly confused and hopeless reasons for killing. Once again a compelling example of how we live parallel lives!

The Tree that Bleeds: A Uighur Town on the Edge

Nick Holdstock

ISBN 978-1906817-64-0 PBK £9.99

In 1997 a small town in a remote part of China was shaken by violent protests that led to the imposition of martial law. Some said it was a peaceful demonstration that was brutally suppressed by the government; others that it was an act of terrorism. When Nick Holdstock arrived in 2001, the town was still bitterly divided. The main resentment was between the Uighurs (an ethnic minority in the region) and the Han (the ethnic majority in China). Living there, Holdstock discovered the political, economic and religious sources of conflict between these different communities, which would later result in the terrible violence of July 2009, when hundreds died in further riots in the region. *The Tree That Bleeds* is a book about what happens when people stop believing their government will listen.

full of good writing and acute observation JOHN GITTINGS, FORMER EAST ASIA CORRESPONDENT, THE GUARDIAN

Peak Water: Civilisation and the World's Water Crisis

Alexander Bell

ISBN 978-1906817-19-0 HBK £16.99

Peak water is the point when the available water is not enough to meet the demands of the world's growing population. We might live on a watery world, but we are exhausting accessible supplies. Many parts of the world are already facing this crisis, and not only in the developing world. Some of the places experiencing 'peak water' are in the USA, Europe and the UK. Even the wettest lands will be engulfed in the global catastrophe that looms – this is the issue of our age.

Alexander Bell shows how water control flows through politics, religion, farming and the idea of the modern state. Yet history is littered with empires that have failed and vanished into dust, and Bell argues that we might face a similar fate unless we learn to manage our water better.

an eloquent and alarmingly persuasive book THE SCOTSMAN

The Fatal Sleep
Peter Kennedy
ISBN 978-1906817480 PBK £9.99

The bite of the tsetse fly – a burning sting into the skin – causes a descent into violent fever and aching pains. Severe bouts of insomnia are followed by mental deterioration, disruption of the nervous system, coma and ultimately death.

Sleeping sickness, also known as human African trypanosomiasis, is one of Africa's major killers. It puts 60 million people at risk of infection and occurs in 36 countries in sub-Saharan Africa. The disease claims the lives of many thousands of people every year, and the toxic effects of the treatment currently available can be as painful and dangerous as the disease itself. Existing in the shadow of malaria and AIDS, it is an overlooked disease, largely ignored by pharmaceutical companies and neglected by the western world.

Highly commended at the BMA Popular Medicine Book Awards.

This is a remarkable book. It is filled in equal measure with passion for science and compassion for the people afflicted with this cruel disease. SIR ROGER BANNISTER

Kennedy is to be congratulated on writing a book for a general audience about an important but neglected tropical disease. BRITISH MEDICAL JOURNAL

From the Ganga to the Tay: A Poetic Conversation between the Ganges and the Tay
Bashabi Fraser and Kenny Munro
ISBN 978-1906307-95-0 PBK £8.99

The mythical qualities of Indian rivers is profound with daily rituals imprinted in community consciousness. Scotland's rivers were also recognised as the life blood of mother earth, and considered sacred, but cultural evolution seems to have clouded our ancestors' respect for Scotland's most powerful river, the Tay. KENNY MUNRO

From the Ganga to the Tay is an epic poem in which the Indian River Ganges and the Scottish River Tay, the largest waterways in their countries, relate the historical importance of the ties between India and Scotland. The rivers are potent natural symbols of continuity and peace. With stunning photographs, the conversation between the rivers explores centuries of shared history between Scotland and India as well as each river's personal journey through time.

In the art of Bashabi Fraser the cultures of India and Scotland richly blend, and in this magnificent poem the two living traditions speak to each other through the riverine oracles of the Ganges and the Tay. RICHARD HOLLOWAY

Trident and International Law: Scotland's Obligations

Edited by Rebecca Johnson and Angie Zelter

ISBN 978-1906817-24-4 PBK £12.99

As a further generation of nuclear-armed submarines is developed, *Trident and International Law* challenges the legality of UK nuclear policy, and asks who is really accountable for Coulport and Faslane.

Although controlled by the Westminster Government, and to some extent by the US Government, all of the UK's nuclear weapons are based in Scotland. The Scottish Government therefore has responsibilities under domestic and international law relating to the deployment of nuclear weapons in Scotland. Public concern expressed over these responsibilities led to the Acronym Institute for Disarmament Diplomacy, the Edinburgh Peace and Justice Centre and Trident Ploughshares organising an international conference, 'Trident and International Law: Scotland's Obligations'. This book presents the major documents and papers, with additional arguments from renowned legal scholars. The conclusions deserve careful consideration.

Gross violations of international obligations are not excluded from the purview of the Scottish Parliament.
H.E. Judge Christopher Weeramantry

Stolen from Africa

Kokumo Rocks

ISBN 978-1906307-19-6 PBK £7.99

Have you ever seen a megalomaniac butterfly throw a hissy fit?
Ever been mown down by a disgruntled lawnmower?
Have you ever noticed that there are no black prosthetic legs?

Kokumo Rock's poetry is a vibrant and energetic foray into a world of absurd situations and vivid imagination. Drawing on all the senses, she expresses anger over war, joy in the natural world, and delights in the silly and strange aspects of life.

While Kokumo expresses her despair over racism and war, in the next moment she will convey the joyful suggestion of a better future. You will laugh at the way she brings life and energy to everyday objects and, above all, relish the refreshing and passionate poetry of Scotland's dynamic African-Asian performance poet as she celebrates and examines her own background.

... similar to Angelou's work, but sharper and more hip. SHEREEN TUOMI

Out of Pocket:
How Collective Amnesia Lost the World its Wealth, Again
Clark McGinn

Gangs of Dundee
Gary Robertson
ISBN 978-1906307-02-8 PBK £9.99

Written by a senior banker with many years' experience, this book takes the long view. It shows how simple the basics of banking are and tells the stories of how we lost money in similar ways over the centuries. Read it and you might just lose less money next time!

If only the world's finance ministers, bank CEOs, non execs, customers, borrowers, little old ladies, all of us, had read this book three years ago, or 30 years ago, we wouldn't be in the mess we're in. But we are. So read this book and weep. And take solace in the fact that financial calamities have happened many many times before, and will happen again.

I started writing this book three years ago to amuse my fellow bankers. Little did we all know what was about to happen. But we should have. Sorry. CLARK McGINN

This is an intriguing book by an experienced banker... the book expresses its themes with literary flair. THE IRISH TIMES

Ye knew wah ah the ither gangs wir, ye knew the colours an ye knew maist o the nuttirz.

No bein associated wi a gang wizna really an option. The law o the street jungle prevailed.

Dundee has a long, illustrious and well-documented history – the city of 'jute, jam and journalism'. There is, however, one aspect of Scotland's fourth largest city yet to be told – the story of Dundee's gangs.

From the Huns to the Shimmy, the Shams and the Fleet, the stories of generation after generation of Dundee's youth's have without doubt been shaped by gang culture. It is this side of Dundee's history that is revealed by former gang member Gary Robertson.

Robertson tells the stories of the gangs in their own words, basing his accounts on interviews with former and current gang members, giving an anecdotal, colourful, and fundamentally true-to-life history of this volatile subject.

Luath Press Limited

committed to publishing well written books worth reading

LUATH PRESS takes its name from Robert Burns, whose little collie Luath (*Gael.*, swift or nimble) tripped up Jean Armour at a wedding and gave him the chance to speak to the woman who was to be his wife and the abiding love of his life. Burns called one of the 'Twa Dogs' Luath after Cuchullin's hunting dog in Ossian's *Fingal*.

Luath Press was established in 1981 in the heart of Burns country, and is now based a few steps up the road from Burns' first lodgings on Edinburgh's Royal Mile. Luath offers you distinctive writing with a hint of unexpected pleasures.

Most bookshops in the UK, the US, Canada, Australia, New Zealand and parts of Europe, either carry our books in stock or can order them for you. To order direct from us, please send a £sterling cheque, postal order, international money order or your credit card details (number, address of cardholder and expiry date) to us at the address below. Please add post and packing as follows: UK – £1.00 per delivery address; overseas surface mail – £2.50 per delivery address; overseas airmail – £3.50 for the first book to each delivery address, plus £1.00 for each additional book by airmail to the same address. If your order is a gift, we will happily enclose your card or message at no extra charge.

Luath Press Limited
543/2 Castlehill
The Royal Mile
Edinburgh EH1 2ND
Scotland
Telephone: +44 (0)131 225 4326 (24 hours)
Fax: +44 (0)131 225 4324
email: sales@luath. co.uk
Website: www. luath.co.uk

ROGER HUNT is from the North East of Scotland and has spent the majority of his career working in management positions within the Royal Bank of Scotland. In 2008 Roger was caught up in the terrorist attacks in Mumbai, and knows just how miraculous it was that he came out of the flame-swept Oberoi Trident Hotel alive. Roger left RBS to join the Scottish Prison Service, where he was HR Manager for HMP Peterhead and HMP Aberdeen for almost two years. He currently works for British Airport Authority (BAA) as Head of Human Resources based in Aberdeen airport. Following the attacks, Roger has shared some of his experiences live on STV's *The Hour*, spoken at Grampian Police's Annual Conference and been regularly involved in activities supporting Counter Terrorism. Roger lives in Macduff with his wife and three children. *Be Silent or Be Killed* is his first book.